D0832750

COOKSHELF

Fish &
Seafood

Carol Tennant

This is a Parragon Book
First published in 2001

Parragon
Queen Street House
4 Queen Street
Bath BA1 1HE, UK

Copyright © Parragon 2001

All rights reserved. No part of this publication may be reproduced, stored
in a retrieval system or transmitted, in any form or by any means, electronic,
mechanical, photocopying, recording or otherwise, without the prior permission
of the copyright holder.

Hardback ISBN: 0-75254-963-4
Paperback ISBN: 0-75254-984-7

Printed in China

NOTE

This book uses metric and imperial measurements.
Follow the same units of measurement throughout; do not mix metric and imperial.
All spoon measurements are level: teaspoons are assumed to be 5 ml, and tablespoons are assumed to be 15 ml.
Unless otherwise stated, milk is assumed to be full fat, eggs and individual vegetables
such as potatoes are medium, and pepper is freshly ground black pepper.

Recipes using raw or very lightly cooked eggs should be avoided by infants, the elderly,
pregnant women, convalescents, and anyone suffering from an illness.

Contents

Introduction

Seafood rightly deserves its image as a healthy food. It is high in protein and with the added bonus of oily fish, such as mackerel and herring, being high in polyunsaturated fat – this is the one that helps reduce cholesterol levels. White fish are a good source of minerals as well as being low in fat, especially if poached, steamed or lightly grilled. Although shellfish have been linked with high cholesterol, they are also low in saturated fats and are therefore fine eaten in moderation. The sheer variety of fish and shellfish is staggering. If you decided to eat seafood just once a week, you could go for a whole year without eating the same dish twice. Seafood is also quick and easy to prepare, making it an attractive ingredient to the busy cook. Often sold ready-to-cook, fish can be prepared in minutes and most shellfish is sold already cooked, needing even less preparation.

Fish is also very good value for money compared to meat, as there is much less waste and no fat or gristle to contend with. Therefore making fish a regular part of your diet makes a lot of sense.

BUYING FISH AND SHELLFISH

Wherever you are shopping for fish – at your local trusted fishmonger or supermarket – the guidelines are the same:

• The eyes of the fish should be clear, bright and moist. Fish with dull, grey or cloudy eyes should be avoided.

• The gills of the fish should be bright red or pin and never dull and grey.

• The fish should smell of the sea and nothing else.

• If you press the fish lightly with your thumb, the flesh should spring back, leaving little or no imprint.

• The shells of hinged shellfish, such as oysters, mussels and clams, should be tightly closed before cooking. If they are slightly open, tap them sharply. If they do not close, discard them.

• Cooked shellfish should smell fresh, with no hint of ammonia. If available, check the use-by-date.

STORING

As you never know how long ago the fish was caught, especially in a supermarket, it is best to buy fish and cook it on the same day. Unfortunately, modern refrigerators are not ideal places to store fish as they tend to have a temperature of about 5°C/38°F and fish is best kept at 0°C/32°F. If you have to keep fish, don't keep it for more than one or two days. Put the fish into a plastic container and scatter over some ice. Cover with cling film and keep in the coldest part of the refrigerator.

Firmer-fleshed fish, such as turbot, Dover sole and monkfish, freeze better than less firm-fleshed fish, such as bass, lemon sole and plaice, but all will deteriorate over a relatively short period. Oily fish is the least successful when frozen. However, if you have to keep your fish for more than a day or two, then freezing is the best option. Ensure that you thaw fish thoroughly and slowly before cooking.

PREPARATION

How much preparation your fish needs depends on where you buy it. Supermarkets may have a wet fish counter with a trained fishmonger on hand while others sell their fish vacuum-packed. Many fish are sold already scaled and gutted, and are often available either whole or filleted. It is usually cheaper, however, to buy a whole fish and prepare it yourself. A fishmonger will usually do this job for you for the price of a whole fish. However, it is not difficult to do yourself and only takes a sharp knife and some practice.

EQUIPMENT

Although, in general, you don't need a great deal of specialist equipment, there are a few items you might consider if you plan on cooking a lot of fish. If, for example, you are planning on poaching whole fish, then a wise investment would be a fish kettle. This is an oblong stainless steel pan with a lifter and lid. They are usually available in several sizes.

A wok or large, heavy-based frying pan is useful for frying and stir-frying. If you like to steam fish you might like to consider a double boiler, bamboo steamer or electric steamer. A thermometer is useful when you are deep-frying, as is a deep-frying basket and large pan.

If you intend cleaning your own fish, a good filleting knife is a must. Tweezers are also useful for removing small bones. Different fish suit different cooking methods but, as a general rule, poaching, steaming and stewing tend to produce moister results than grilling, baking or barbecuing.

Drying out can be minimized, however, if the latter three methods are used at sufficiently high temperatures to reduce moisture loss by cooking the fish very quickly.

COOKING METHODS

POACHING

The fish is immersed in a poaching liquid, which might be a court-bouillon, fish stock, milk, beer or cider. Bring the liquid to the boil and as soon as it boils, remove the pan from the heat and leave the fish to finish cooking in the residual heat. This method helps to prevent overcooking and is also excellent if you want to serve the fish cold

STEAMING

Both fish and shellfish benefit from being steamed. Again, a flavoured liquid can be used for the steaming, which will impart some of its flavour to the fish as it is being cooked. This method is especially good for keeping the fish moist and the flavour delicate. Steaming can be done in a fish kettle, double boiler or steamer inserted over a pan of boiling water.

STEWING

Either whole fish or smaller pieces can be cooked in liquid along with other ingredients, such as vegetables, as a stew. The fish flavours the liquid as it cooks, giving a distinctive taste.

GRILLING

This is one of the quickest and easiest cooking methods for fish. Cook either whole fish, steaks or fillets. Shellfish can also be grilled, but may need halving lengthways first. Whatever you are cooking, ensure that the grill is on its highest setting and that the fish is cooked as close to the heat source as possible. A barbecue is also a very useful tool for grilling fish. Brush the fish with butter, oil or a marinade before and during cooking to ensure that the flesh remains moist.

BAKING AND ROASTING

This covers all methods of cooking in the oven, including open roasting, casseroling or *en papillote*. This is a good method to choose for entertaining because, once the dish is in the oven, you are free to attend to other things.

DEEP-FRYING

The fish is either coated in batter, flour or breadcrumbs and deep-fried in oil. You need a large, heavy-based saucepan or a deep-fryer. Large pieces of fish in batter are best cooked at a lower temperature of 180°C/350°F which allows the fish to cook without burning the batter. Smaller pieces of fish, such as goujons in breadcrumbs, should be cooked at a higher temperature of 190°C/375°F. Drain deep-fried items on kitchen paper to ensure that they remain crisp.

SHALLOW OR PAN FRYING

This is a quick method for cooking fish and shellfish and can take as little as 3–4 minutes. A shallow layer of oil or butter and oil is heated in a frying pan, the fish added and cooked until just tender and lightly browned. A good non-stick frying pan is an essential piece of equipment.

The argument for increasing the amount of fish and seafood in our diets is compelling. Fish and seafood can provide variety, versatility, creativity and luxury as well as being much healthier than meat. Why not give it a try?

Starters & Appetizers

The dishes in this chapter are designed either to whet the appetite for the main course to come, without being filling, or as nibbles to serve with drinks. Fish and seafood make excellent starters as they are full of flavour and can be turned into a variety of delicious dishes. Fish is also much lighter than meat and therefore won't be overly filling.

Fish cooks quickly, making it ideal for entertaining. Many of the dishes in this chapter can be prepared in advance and served cold, such as the Anchovy Bites, the Smoked Mackerel Pâté and the Lime & Basil Cured Salmon, or simply reheated, like the Curried Mussel Tartlets or the Stuffed Squid.

There is also a good selection of first course options, for example the Thai Crab Omelette, Potted Shrimps and Maryland Crab Cakes with Basil & Tomato Dressing, and lots of lovely salad ideas, including the Smoked Haddock Salad and the Bruschetta with Anchoiade, Mixed Tomatoes & Mozzarella.

Anchovy Bites

Makes: about 30

INGREDIENTS

175 g/6 oz plain flour	ANCHOIADE	1 tbsp roughly chopped
6 tbsp butter, cut into	2 x 50 g/1¾ oz cans anchovy	fresh basil
small pieces	fillets in olive oil, drained	1 tbsp lemon juice
4 tbsp freshly grated	100 ml/3½ fl oz milk	2 tbsp blanched almonds, toasted
Parmesan cheese	2 garlic cloves, roughly chopped	and roughly chopped
3 tbsp Dijon mustard	1 tbsp roughly chopped fresh	4 tbsp olive oil
salt and pepper	flat-leaved parsley	

1 To make the pastry, sieve the flour into a large bowl and add the butter. Rub together until the mixture resembles breadcrumbs. Stir in half the Parmesan cheese and salt. Add enough cold water (about 3 tablespoons) to form a firm dough. Knead briefly, wrap in cling film and chill in the refrigerator for 30 minutes.

2 Meanwhile, make the anchoiade. Put the drained anchovies into a small bowl and pour over the milk to cover. Leave to soak for 10 minutes. Drain the anchovies and pat dry on kitchen paper. Discard the milk.

3 Roughly chop the anchovies and put into a food processor or blender with the garlic, parsley, basil, lemon juice, almonds and 2 tablespoons of the oil. Blend until smooth. Scrape out of the food processor or blender and stir in the remaining olive oil and pepper to taste. Set aside.

4 Remove the pastry from the refrigerator and roll out very thinly to a large rectangle measuring 55 x 37.5 cm/20 x 15 inches. Spread thinly with 2 tbsp of the anchoiade and the Dijon mustard. Sprinkle over the remaining Parmesan cheese and some black pepper.

5 Starting from a long edge, roll up tightly then slice crossways into 1 cm/½ in thick slices. Arrange cut side up and well spaced on a non-stick baking tray.

6 Place in a preheated oven at 200°C/400°F/Gas Mark 6 for 20 minutes until golden. Cool on a wire rack.

Bruschetta with Anchoiade, Mixed Tomatoes & Mozzarella

Serves 4

INGREDIENTS

2 x 150 g/5½ oz balls buffalo
    mozzarella, drained
115 g/4 oz orange
    cherry tomatoes
115 g/4 oz red cherry tomatoes
2 ripe plum or red beef tomatoes

2 ripe orange or yellow
    beef tomatoes
4 tbsp extra-virgin olive oil, plus
    extra for drizzling
1 tbsp balsamic vinegar
8 thick slices ciabatta or other
    rustic country bread

1 garlic clove
4 tbsp Anchoiade (see page 8)
handful basil leaves
salt and pepper

1 Slice the mozzarella balls into thick slices. Set aside. Halve the cherry tomatoes and thickly slice the plum and beef tomatoes.

2 To make the dressing, whisk together the olive oil, balsamic vinegar and seasoning.

3 Toast the bread on both sides, then rub one side with the garlic clove. Drizzle with a little olive oil. Spread the Anchoiade on the toasts.

4 To assemble the salad, arrange the sliced tomatoes on each of 4 serving plates and scatter with cherry tomatoes.

5 Top the toasts with the slices of mozzarella cheese and 2–3 halved cherry tomatoes. Cook the toasts under a preheated grill for about 3–4 minutes until softened. Drizzle over the dressing and scatter with fresh basil leaves. Season to taste with black pepper.

6 Put 2 slices of toast on the plates and serve.

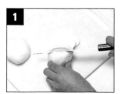

Bagna Cauda with Crudités

Serves 8

INGREDIENTS

1 yellow pepper
3 celery sticks
2 carrots
115 g/4 oz mushrooms
½ cauliflower
1 fennel bulb
1 bunch spring onions

2 beetroot, cooked
    and peeled
8 radishes
225 g/8 oz boiled
    new potatoes
225 ml/8 fl oz olive oil
5 garlic cloves, crushed

50 g/1¾ oz can anchovies in oil,
    drained and chopped
115 g/4 oz butter
Italian bread, to serve

1 Prepare the vegetables. Deseed and thickly slice the pepper. Cut the celery into 7.5 cm/3 in lengths. Cut the carrots into batons. Score the mushrooms with 4 cuts like spokes on a wheel. Separate the cauliflower into florets. Cut the fennel in half lengthways, then cut each half into 4 lengthways. Trim the spring onions. Cut the beetroot into eighths. Trim the radishes. Cut the potatoes in half, if large. Arrange the prepared vegetables on a large serving platter.

2 Heat the oil very gently in a saucepan. Add the garlic and anchovies and cook very gently, stirring, until the anchovies have disintegrated. Take care not to brown or burn the garlic.

3 Add the butter and as soon as it has melted, serve straight away with the selection of crudités and plenty of bread.

COOK'S TIP

If you have one, a fondue set is perfect for serving this dish as the sauce can be kept hot at the table.

Giant Garlic Prawns

Serves 4

INGREDIENTS

125 ml/4 fl oz olive oil
4 garlic cloves, finely chopped
2 hot red chillies, deseeded and
    finely chopped

450 g/1 lb cooked king prawns
2 tbsp chopped fresh
    flat-leaved parsley
salt and pepper

lemon wedges, to garnish
crusty bread, to serve

1 Heat the oil in a large frying pan over a low heat. Add the garlic and chillies and cook for 1–2 minutes until softened but not coloured.

2 Add the prawns and stir-fry for 2–3 minutes until heated through and coated in the oil and garlic mixture. Remove from the heat.

3 Add the parsley and stir well to mix. Season to taste with salt and pepper.

4 Divide the prawns and garlicky oil between warmed serving dishes and garnish with lemon wedges. Serve with lots of fresh crusty bread.

COOK'S TIP

If you can get hold of raw prawns, cook them as above but increase the cooking time to 5–6 minutes until the prawns are cooked through and turn bright pink.

Mini Prawn Spring Rolls

Makes about 30

INGREDIENTS

50 g/1¼ oz dried rice vermicelli
1 carrot, cut into matchsticks
50 g/1¼ oz mangetouts,
    shredded thinly lengthways
3 spring onions, finely chopped
100 g/3½ oz cooked
    peeled prawns

2 garlic cloves, crushed
1 tsp sesame oil
2 tbsp light soy sauce
1 tsp chilli sauce
200 g/7 oz filo pastry, cut into
    15 cm/6 inch squares

1 egg white, beaten
vegetable oil, for deep-frying
dark soy sauce, sweet chilli sauce
    or Sweet and Sour Dipping
    Sauce (see page 40),
    for dipping

1 Cook the rice vermicelli according to the packet instructions. Drain thoroughly. Roughly chop and set aside. Bring a pan of salted water to the boil and blanch the carrot and mangetouts for 1 minute. Drain and refresh under cold water. Drain again and pat dry on kitchen paper. Mix together with the noodles and add the spring onions, prawns, garlic, sesame oil, soy sauce and chilli sauce. Set aside.

2 Fold the filo pastry squares in half diagonally to form triangles. Lay a triangle on the work surface, with the fold facing you, and place a spoonful of the mixture in the centre. Roll over the wrapper to enclose the filling, then bring over the corners to enclose the ends of the roll. Brush the point of the spring roll furthest from you with a little beaten egg white and continue rolling to seal. Continue with the remaining filo triangles to make about 30 spring rolls.

3 Fill a deep-fryer or saucepan about a third full with vegetable oil and heat to 190°C/375°F or until a cube of bread browns in 30 seconds. Fry the spring rolls, 4 or 5 at a time, for 1–2 minutes or until golden and crisp. Drain on kitchen paper. Fry the remaining spring rolls in batches.

4 Serve hot with dark soy sauce, sweet chilli sauce or Sweet and Sour Sauce for dipping.

Prawn Satay

Serves 4

INGREDIENTS

12 peeled raw king prawns	125 ml/4 fl oz coconut milk	225 ml/8 fl oz fish or
	3 tbsp sugar	chicken stock
MARINADE		1 tbsp sugar
1 tsp ground coriander	PEANUT SAUCE	1 tsp salt
1 tsp ground cumin	2 tbsp vegetable oil	1 tbsp lemon juice
2 tbsp light soy sauce	3 garlic cloves, crushed	4 tbsp unsalted roasted peanuts,
4 tbsp vegetable oil	1 tbsp red curry paste (see	finely chopped
1 tbsp curry powder	page 102)	4 tbsp dried breadcrumbs
1 tbsp ground turmeric	125 ml/4 fl oz coconut milk	

1 Slit the prawns down their backs and remove the black vein, if any. Set aside. Mix together the marinade ingredients and add the prawns. Mix together well, cover and set aside for at least 8 hours or overnight.

2 To make the peanut sauce, heat the oil in a large frying pan until very hot. Add the garlic and fry until just starting to colour. Add the curry paste and mix together well, cooking for a further 30 seconds. Add the coconut milk, stock, sugar, salt and lemon juice and stir well. Boil for 1–2 minutes, stirring constantly. Add the peanuts and breadcrumbs and mix together well. Pour the sauce into a serving bowl and set aside.

3 Using 4 skewers, thread 3 prawns on to each. Cook under a preheated hot grill or on the barbecue for 3–4 minutes on each side until just cooked through. Serve immediately with the peanut sauce.

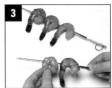

Potted Shrimps

Serves 4

INGREDIENTS

225 g/8 oz unsalted butter
400 g/14 oz brown shrimps
in their shells or 225 g/8 oz
cooked peeled prawns

pinch of cayenne pepper
½ tsp ground mace
1 garlic clove, crushed
1 tbsp chopped fresh parsley

salt and pepper
lemon wedges and fresh parsley
sprigs, to garnish
brown bread, to serve

1 Heat the butter in a small saucepan until melted and foaming. Set aside for 10 minutes or until the butter separates. Carefully skim off the clear yellow liquid and discard the white milk solids. The clear yellow oil remaining is clarified butter.

2 Peel the shrimps, if necessary, discarding the shells. Heat 2 tablespoons of the clarified butter in a frying pan and add the shrimps. Stir in the cayenne, mace and garlic. Increase the heat and stir-fry for 30 seconds until

very hot. Remove from the heat, stir in the parsley and season to taste.

3 Divide the shrimps between 4 small ramekins, pressing down with the back of a spoon. Pour over the remaining clarified butter to cover. Refrigerate until the butter has set.

4 Remove the ramekins from the refrigerator 30 minutes before serving to allow the butter to soften. Toast the brown bread and serve with the shrimps,

garnished with lemon wedges and fresh parsley sprigs if liked.

COOK'S TIP

The most authentic shrimps to use for this recipe are the tiny brown shrimps. They have a full flavour and soak up the butter well. If your fishmonger can't supply them, substitute the pink peeled variety.

Prunes Stuffed with Mussels

Makes 24

INGREDIENTS

3 tbsp port
1 tbsp clear honey
2 garlic cloves, crushed

24 large stoned prunes
24 live mussels

12 rashers smoked streaky bacon
salt and pepper

1 Mix together the port, honey and garlic, then season with salt and pepper. Put the prunes into a small bowl and pour over the port mixture. Cover and leave to marinate for at least 4 hours and preferably overnight.

2 Next day, clean the mussels by scrubbing or scraping the shells and pulling off any beards. Put the mussels in a large saucepan with just the water that clings to their shells. Cook, covered, over a high heat for 3–4 minutes until all the mussels have opened. Discard any mussels that remain closed.

3 Drain the mussels, reserving the cooking liquid. Allow to cool, then remove the mussels from their shells.

4 Using the back of a knife, stretch the bacon rashers then cut in half widthways. Lift the prunes from their marinade, reserving any that remains.

5 Stuff each prune with a mussel, then wrap with a piece of bacon. Secure with a cocktail stick. Repeat to make 24.

6 In a saucepan, simmer together the mussel cooking liquid and remaining marinade until reduced and syrupy. Brush the stuffed prunes with this mixture. Place under a preheated grill and cook for 3–4 minutes each side, turning regularly and brushing with the marinade, until the bacon is crisp and golden. Serve while still hot.

VARIATION

As an alternative to smoked bacon use pancetta or Parma ham, cut into strips, instead and cook as above.

Mussel Fritters

Serves 4–6

INGREDIENTS

175 g/6 oz plain flour
pinch of salt
1 egg
225 ml/8 fl oz lager
900 g/2 lb live mussels
vegetable oil, for deep-frying

GARLIC AND HERB MAYONNAISE
1 egg yolk
1 tsp Dijon mustard
1 tsp white wine vinegar
2 tbsp chopped fresh mixed
    herbs, such as parsley, chives,
    basil, thyme

2 garlic cloves, crushed
225 ml/8 fl oz olive oil
salt and pepper

TO GARNISH
lemon slices
fresh parsley

1 To make the batter, put the flour into a bowl with a pinch of salt. Add the egg and half the lager and whisk until smooth. Gradually add the remaining lager, whisking until smooth. Set aside for 30 minutes.

2 Clean the mussels by scrubbing or scraping the shells and pulling off any beards that are attached to them. Discard any with broken shells or any that refuse to close when tapped. Put the mussels into a large pan with just the water on their shells and cook, covered, over a high heat for 3–4 minutes, shaking the pan occasionally, until all the mussels have opened. Discard any mussels that remain closed. Drain and set aside until cool enough to handle, then remove the mussels from their shells.

3 To make the garlic and herb mayonnaise, process the egg yolk, mustard, vinegar, herbs, garlic and seasoning to taste. in a food processor or blender until frothy. With the motor still running, add the olive oil, drop by drop to begin with, until the mixture begins to thicken. Continue adding the oil in a thin, steady stream. Add a little hot water if the mixture seems too thick. Set aside.

4 Meanwhile, fill a deep saucepan about a third full with vegetable oil and heat to 190°C/375°F or until a cube of bread browns in 30 seconds. Drop the mussels, a few at a time, into the batter and lift out with a slotted spoon. Drop into the hot oil and cook for 1–2 minutes until the batter is crisp and golden. Drain thoroughly on kitchen paper. Serve the mussel fritters hot with the garlic and herb mayonnaise and garnished with lemon slices and parsley.

Mussels with Pesto

Serves 4

INGREDIENTS

900g/2 lb live mussels
6 tbsp chopped fresh basil
2 garlic cloves, crushed
1 tbsp pine kernels, toasted
2 tbsp freshly grated
   Parmesan cheese

100 ml/3½ fl oz olive oil
115 g/4 oz fresh
   white breadcrumbs
salt and pepper

TO GARNISH
basil leaves
tomato slices

1 Clean the mussels by scrubbing or scraping the shells and pulling off any beards that are attached to them. Discard any with broken shells or any that refuse to close when tapped. Put the mussels into a large pan with just the water on their shells and cook, covered, over a high heat for 3–4 minutes, shaking the pan occasionally, until all the mussels have opened. Discard any mussels that remain closed. Drain, reserving the cooking liquid, and set aside until cool enough to handle.

2 Strain the cooking liquid into a clean pan and simmer until reduced to about 1 tablespoon. Put the liquid into a food processor with the basil, garlic, pine kernels and Parmesan and process until finely chopped. Add the olive oil and breadcrumbs and process until well mixed.

3 Open the mussels and loosen them from their shells, discarding the empty half of the shell. Divide the pesto breadcrumbs between the mussels.

4 Cook under a preheated grill until the topping is crisp and golden and the mussels are heated through. Serve immediately garnished with with slices of tomato and basil leaves.

VARIATION

If you want an alternative to pine kernels, add 85 g/3 oz roughly chopped, drained sun-dried tomatoes in oil to the pesto instead.

Curried Mussel Tartlets

Serves 6

INGREDIENTS

175 g/6 oz plain flour	CURRIED MUSSEL FILLING	200 ml/7 fl oz double cream
½ tsp ground turmeric	450 g/1 lb live mussels	2 egg yolks
½ tsp salt	2 tsp vegetable oil	2 tbsp chopped fresh coriander
85 g/3 oz butter	2 garlic cloves, finely chopped	salt and pepper
4 tbsp finely chopped walnuts	1 tsp grated fresh root ginger	
2 tbsp iced water	1 tsp mild curry paste	

1 To make the pastry, sift the flour, turmeric and salt into a bowl. Rub in the butter with your fingers until the mixture resembles fine breadcrumbs. Stir in the walnuts and add the water. Mix briefly until the dough starts to come together, adding a little more water if necessary. Turn the dough on to a lightly floured surface and knead briefly until smooth. Wrap in cling film and chill for 30 minutes.

2 Clean the mussels by scrubbing or scraping the shells and pulling off any beards. Discard any with broken shells or that do not close when tapped. Put the mussels into a large pan with just the water on their shells and cook, covered, over a high heat for 3–4 minutes, shaking the pan occasionally, until all the mussels have opened. Discard any that remain closed. Drain and set aside until cool enough to handle. Remove the mussels from their shells.

3 Heat the oil in a small pan and stir-fry the garlic and ginger for 1 minute. Stir in the curry paste. Remove from the heat and add the cream. Set aside to cool.

4 Divide the pastry into 6 equal pieces. Roll out each piece thinly and use to line 6 x 9 cm/3½ in individual tartlet tins. Carefully line the pastry with foil and fill with baking beans. Place in a preheated oven, 200°C/400°F/Gas Mark 6, for 10 minutes. Remove the foil and beans and cook for a further 5 minutes. Remove from the oven and allow to cool slightly. Reduce the oven temperature to 180°C/350°F/Gas Mark 4.

5 Divide the cooked mussels between the cooled pastry cases. Whisk the egg yolks and coriander into the cooled cream mixture. Then season with salt and pepper to taste and pour the mixture into the pastry cases to cover the mussels. Bake in the preheated oven for 25 minutes until the filling has just set and the pastry is golden. Allow to cool and serve warm with salad.

Calamari

Serves 4

INGREDIENTS

115 g/4 oz plain flour
1 tsp salt
2 eggs
175 ml/6 fl oz soda water

450 g/1 lb prepared squid (see
    method), cut into rings
vegetable oil, for deep-frying

TO GARNISH
lemon wedges
parsley sprigs

1 Sift the flour into a bowl with the salt. Add the eggs and half the soda water and whisk together until smooth. Gradually whisk in the remaining soda water until the batter is smooth. Set aside.

2 To prepare whole squid, hold the body firmly and grasp the tentacles just inside the body. Pull firmly to remove the innards. Find the transparent quill and remove. Grasp the wings on the outside of the body and pull to remove the outer skin. Trim the tentacles just below the beak and reserve.

3 Wash the body and tentacles under running water. Slice the body across into 1 cm/½ in rings. Drain well on kitchen paper.

4 Meanwhile, fill a deep saucepan about a third full with vegetable oil and heat to 190°F/ 375°F or until a cube of bread browns in 30 seconds.

5 Dip the squid rings and tentacles into the batter, a few at a time, and drop into the hot oil. Fry for 1–2 minutes until crisp and golden. Drain on kitchen paper. Cook all the squid this way. Serve immediately while still hot, garnished with lemon wedges and parsley.

COOK'S TIP

If you don't like the idea of cleaning squid yourself, get your fishmonger to do it. Squid is frequently sold already cut into rings. Alternatively, you could use prepared baby squid for this dish.

Stuffed Squid

Serves 4

INGREDIENTS

12 baby squid, cleaned	1 tbsp pine kernels, toasted	25 g/1 oz sun-dried tomatoes in
4 tbsp olive oil	1 tbsp chopped fresh	oil, drained and finely chopped
1 small onion, finely chopped	flat-leaved parsley	125 ml/4 fl oz dry white wine
1 garlic clove, finely chopped	400 g/14 oz canned	salt and pepper
40g /1½ oz basmati rice	chopped tomatoes	crusty bread, to serve
1 tbsp seedless raisins		

1 Separate the tentacles from the body of the squid. Chop the tentacles and set aside. Rub the squid tubes inside and out with 1 teaspoon salt and set aside.

2 Heat 1 tablespoon of the olive oil in a frying pan and add the onion and garlic. Cook over a low heat, stirring occasionally, for 4–5 minutes until softened and lightly browned. Add the chopped tentacles and fry for 2–3 minutes. Add the rice, raisins, pine kernels and parsley and season to taste. Remove from the heat.

3 Allow the rice mixture to cool slightly and spoon it into the squid tubes, about three quarters full to allow the rice to expand. You may need to open the squid tubes a little by making a small cut. Secure each filled squid with a cocktail stick.

4 Heat the remaining oil in a large flameproof casserole. Add the squid and fry for a few minutes on all sides until lightly browned. Add the tomatoes, sun-dried tomatoes, wine and seasoning. Bake in a preheated oven,

180°C/350°F/Gas Mark 4, for 45 minutes. Serve hot or cold with plenty of crusty bread.

COOK'S TIP

If you have difficulty finding baby squid, larger ones work very well and the cooking time is the same. Use cleaned squid weighing 225 g/8 oz in total for the amount of stuffing in this recipe.

Tempura Whitebait

Serves 4

INGREDIENTS

450 g/1 lb whitebait,
   defrosted if frozen
100 g/3½ oz plain flour
50 g/1¾ oz cornflour
½ tsp salt

200 ml/7 fl oz cold water
1 egg
a few ice cubes
vegetable oil, for deep-frying

CHILLI AND LIME MAYONNAISE
1 egg yolk
1 tbsp lime juice
1 fresh red chilli, deseeded and
   finely chopped
2 tbsp chopped fresh coriander
200 ml/7 fl oz light olive oil
salt and pepper

1 To make the mayonnaise, in the bowl of a food processor or blender, mix together the egg yolk, lime juice, chilli, coriander and seasoning until foaming. With the motor running, gradually add the olive oil, drop by drop to begin with, until the mixture begins to thicken. Continue adding the oil in a thin steady stream. Adjust the seasoning and add a little hot water if the mixture seems too thick. Set aside in the refrigerator.

2 For the tempura whitebait, wash and dry the fish. Set aside on kitchen paper. In a large bowl, sift together the plain flour, cornflour and salt. Whisk together the water, egg and ice cubes and pour on to the flour. Whisk briefly until the mixture is runny, but still lumpy with dry bits of flour still apparent.

3 Meanwhile, fill a deep saucepan about a third full with vegetable oil and heat to 190°F/ 375°F or until a cube of bread browns in 30 seconds.

4 Dip the whitebait, a few at a time, into the batter and carefully drop into the hot oil. Fry for 1 minute until the batter is crisp but not browned. Drain on kitchen paper. Cook all the whitebait this way. Serve hot with the chilli and lime mayonnaise.

Smoked Mackerel Pâté

Serves 4

INGREDIENTS

200g /7 oz smoked mackerel fillet
1 small, hot green chilli, deseeded
    and chopped
1 garlic clove, chopped

3 tbsp fresh coriander leaves
150 ml/5 fl oz soured cream
1 small red onion, chopped
2 tbsp lime juice
salt and pepper

MELBA TOAST
4 slices white bread,
    crusts removed

1 Skin and flake the mackerel fillet, removing any small bones. Put the flesh in the bowl of a food processor, together with the chilli, garlic, coriander and soured cream. Blend together until smooth.

2 Transfer the mixture to a bowl and mix in the onion and lime juice. Season to taste with salt and pepper. The pâté will seem very soft at this stage, but it will firm up when chilled in the refrigerator. Chill for several hours or overnight.

3 To make the melba toasts, place the trimmed bread slices under a preheated medium grill and toast lightly on both sides. Split the toasts in half horizontally using a sharp knife, then cut each across diagonally to form 4 triangles per slice.

4 Put the triangles, untoasted side up, under the grill and toast until golden and beginning to curl at the edges. Serve warm or cold with the smoked mackerel pâté.

COOK'S TIP

This pâté is also very good served with vegetable crudities.

Smoked Haddock Salad

Serves 4

INGREDIENTS

350 g/12 oz smoked
    haddock fillets
4 tbsp olive oil
1 tbsp lemon juice
2 tbsp soured cream

1 tbsp hot water
2 tbsp chopped fresh chives, plus
    extra to garnish
1 plum tomato, peeled, deseeded
    and diced

8 quail's eggs
4 thick slices granary or
    multigrain bread
115 g/4 oz mixed salad leaves
salt and pepper

1 Fill a large frying pan with water and bring to the boil. Add the smoked haddock fillet, cover and remove from the heat. Set aside for 10 minutes until the fish is tender. Lift from the poaching water, drain and leave until cool enough to handle. Flake the flesh, removing any small bones. Set aside. Discard the poaching water.

2 Whisk together the olive oil, lemon juice, soured cream, hot water, chives and seasoning. Stir in the tomato. Set aside.

3 Bring a small saucepan of water to the boil. Carefully lower the quail's eggs into the water. Cook the eggs for 3–4 minutes from when the water returns to the boil (3 minutes for a slightly soft centre, 4 minutes for a firm centre). Drain immediately and refresh under cold running water. Carefully peel the eggs, cut in half lengthways and set aside.

4 Toast the bread and cut each slice diagonally to form 4 triangles. Arrange 2 halves on 4 serving plates. Top with the salad leaves, then the flaked fish and finally the quail's egg halves. Spoon over the dressing and garnish with a few extra chives.

COOK'S TIP

When buying smoked haddock, and smoked fish in general, look for undyed fish, which is always superior in quality.

Thai Fish Cakes with Sweet & Sour Chilli Dipping Sauce

Serves 4

INGREDIENTS

450 g/1 lb firm white fish filets, such as hake, haddock or cod, skinned and roughly chopped
1 tbsp Thai fish sauce
1 tbsp Red Curry Paste (see page 102)
1 kaffir lime leaf, finely shredded

2 tbsp chopped fresh coriander
1 egg
1 tsp brown sugar
pinch of salt
40 g/1½ oz green beans, thinly sliced crossways
vegetable oil, for shallow frying

SWEET AND SOUR DIPPING SAUCE
4 tbsp sugar
1 tbsp cold water
3 tbsp white rice vinegar
2 small, hot chillies, finely chopped
1 tbsp Thai fish sauce

1 For the fish cakes, put the fish fillets, Thai fish sauce, Red Curry Paste, lime leaf, coriander, egg, sugar and salt into the bowl of a food processor. Process until smooth and thoroughly combined. Scrape into a bowl and stir in the green beans. Set aside.

2 To make the dipping sauce, put the sugar, water and rice vinegar into a small saucepan and heat gently until the sugar has dissolved. Bring to the boil and simmer for 2 minutes. Remove from the heat and stir in the chopped chillies and Thai fish sauce and set aside to cool.

3 Heat a frying pan with enough oil to cover the bottom generously. Divide the fish mixture into 16 little balls. Flatten the balls into little patties and fry in the hot oil for 1–2 minutes each side until golden. Drain on kitchen paper. Serve hot with the dipping sauce.

COOK'S TIP

It isn't necessary to use the most expensive cut of white fish in this recipe, as the other flavours are very strong. Use whatever is cheapest.

Maryland Crab Cakes with Basil & Tomato Dressing

Serves 4

INGREDIENTS

225 g/8 oz potatoes, cut
   into chunks
450 g/1 lb cooked white and
   brown crab meat, defrosted
   if frozen
6 spring onions, finely chopped
1 small red chilli, deseeded and
   finely chopped

3 tbsp mayonnaise
2 tbsp plain flour
1 egg, lightly beaten
115 g/4 oz fresh white
   breadcrumbs
vegetable oil, for shallow frying
salt and pepper
lemon slices and dill, to garnish

DRESSING
5 tbsp olive oil
1 tbsp lemon juice
1 large ripe tomato, peeled,
   deseeded and diced
3 tbsp chopped fresh basil
salt and pepper

1 Cook the potatoes in boiling salted water for 15–20 minutes until tender. Drain well and mash.

2 In a large bowl, mix together the crab meat, spring onions, chilli and mayonnaise. Add the mashed potato and seasoning and mix together well. Shape the mixture into 8 cakes.

3 Put the flour, egg and breadcrumbs into separate bowls. Dip the cakes first into the flour, then into the egg and finally, into the breadcrumbs to coat. Refrigerate for 30 minutes.

4 In a large frying pan, heat enough vegetable oil to cover the bottom of the pan generously. Add the cakes, in batches if necessary, and cook for 3–4 minutes on each side until golden and crisp. Drain on kitchen paper and keep warm.

5 Meanwhile, for the dressing, put the oil, lemon juice and tomato in a small saucepan and heat gently for 2–3 minutes. Remove from the heat, stir in the basil and season to taste with salt and pepper.

6 Divide the fish cakes between 4 individual warmed serving plates. Spoon over the dressing. Serve immediately, garnished with lemon slices and dill.

Lime & Basil Cured Salmon

Serves 6

INGREDIENTS

900 g/2 lb very fresh salmon
    fillet, from the head
    end, skinned
50 g/1¾ oz sugar
50 g/1¾ oz sea salt
5 tbsp chopped fresh basil
finely grated rind of 2 limes
1 tsp white peppercorns,
    lightly crushed

DRESSING
200 ml/7 fl oz rice vinegar
5 tbsp sugar
finely grated rind of 1 lime
½ tsp English mustard
3 tbsp chopped fresh basil
1 tbsp Japanese pickled ginger,
    finely shredded

TO GARNISH
lime wedges
basil leaves

TO SERVE
150 g/5½ oz mixed salad leaves

1 Remove any small pin bones that remain in the salmon fillet. Wash and dry the fish. Place the salmon in a large non-metallic dish and sprinkle evenly with the sugar, sea salt, basil, lime rind and peppercorns. Cover and chill for 24–48 hours, turning the fish occasionally.

2 For the dressing, put the rice vinegar and sugar in a small saucepan and stir gently over a low heat until the sugar has completely dissolved. Then, bring to the boil and simmer for 5–6 minutes until the liquid is reduced by about one-third. Remove the saucepan from the heat and stir in the lime rind and mustard. Set the saucepan aside.

3 Remove the salmon fillet from the marinade, wiping off any excess with kitchen paper. Using a sharp, knife, slice the fish very thinly.

4 To serve, stir the chopped basil and ginger into the dressing. Toss the salad leaves with a little of the dressing and arrange on 6 serving plates. Divide the salmon slices between the plates and drizzle a little dressing over. Garnish with lime wedges and basil leaves and serve immediately.

Hot-smoked Salmon Scramble

Serves 4

INGREDIENTS

50 g/1¾ oz butter, plus extra
    for spreading
8 eggs, lightly beaten
4 tbsp double cream

225 g/8 oz skinless, boneless hot-
    smoked salmon, flaked
2 tbsp chopped fresh mixed
    herbs such as chives, basil
    and parsley

4 muffins, split
salt and pepper
chopped fresh chives, to garnish
lemon wedges, to serve

1 Melt the butter in a large
frying pan and when it
begins to foam, add the eggs.
Leave for a moment to start
to set, then slowly stir and
move the set eggs away from
the bottom of the pan to
allow uncooked egg to take
its place. Leave again for a
moment and repeat.

2 Before all the egg has
set, stir in the double
cream, flaked salmon and
chopped herbs. Stir gently to
incorporate fully. Do not
overcook the eggs.

3 Meanwhile, toast the
split muffins on both
sides. Spread with extra
butter if liked. Place 2 muffin
halves on each of 4 plates.

4 When the eggs are
cooked, divide them
between the muffins.
Sprinkle over a few chopped
chives, season to taste with
salt and pepper and serve
while still warm, garnished
with a. lemon wedge.

VARIATION

*If you have difficulty
finding hot-smoked
salmon, you could
substitute conventional
smoked salmon and
chop rather than flake it.*

Griddled Smoked Salmon

Serves 4

INGREDIENTS

350 g/12 oz sliced
    smoked salmon

DRESSING
1 tsp Dijon mustard
1 garlic clove, crushed

2 tsp chopped fresh dill
2 tsp sherry vinegar
4 tbsp olive oil
salt and pepper
115 g/4 oz mixed salad leaves,
    to serve

1 Take the slices of smoked salmon and fold them, making two folds accordion style, so that they form little parcels.

2 Whisk together the mustard, garlic, dill, vinegar and salt and pepper to taste. Gradually whisk in the olive oil to form a light emulsion. Set aside.

3 Heat a ridged griddle pan until smoking.

Cook the salmon parcels on one side only for 2–3 minutes until heated through and marked from the pan.

4 Meanwhile, dress the salad leaves with some of the vinaigrette and divide between 4 serving plates.

5 Top with the cooked smoked salmon, cooked side up. Drizzle the fish with the remaining dressing and serve immediately.

COOK'S TIP

Smoked salmon is very expensive. This recipe would also work well with smoked trout.

Salmon Tartare

Serves 4

INGREDIENTS

900 g/2 lb very fresh salmon
    fillet, skinned
3 tbsp lemon juice
3 tbsp lime juice
2 tsp sugar
1 tsp Dijon mustard
1 tbsp chopped fresh dill

1 tbsp chopped fresh basil
2 tbsp olive oil
50 g/1¾ oz rocket
handful basil leaves
50 g/1¾ oz mixed salad leaves
salt and pepper

TO GARNISH
dill sprigs
basil leaves

1 Cut the salmon into very tiny dice and season to taste with salt and pepper. Place it in a large, non-metallic bowl.

2 Mix together the lemon juice, lime juice, sugar, mustard, dill, basil and olive oil. Pour over the salmon and mix well. Set aside for 15–20 minutes until the fish becomes opaque.

3 Meanwhile, mix together the rocket, basil leaves and salad leaves. Divide between 4 individual serving plates.

4 To serve the salmon, fill a small ramekin or mini pudding basin with the mixture and turn out on to the centre of the salad leaves. Garnish with dill sprigs and basil leaves.

VARIATION

Haddock also responds very well to this treatment. Use half the quantity of salmon and an equal weight of haddock.

Gravadlax

Serves 6

INGREDIENTS

2 x 450 g/1 lb salmon fillets,
    with skin on
6 tbsp roughly chopped fresh dill
115 g/4 oz sea salt
50 g/1¾ oz sugar

1 tbsp white peppercorns,
    roughly crushed
12 slices brown bread, buttered,
    to serve

TO GARNISH
lemon slices
dill sprigs

1 Wash the salmon fillets in cold running water and pat dry with kitchen paper. Put 1 fillet, skin side down, in a non-metallic dish.

2 Mix together the dill, sea salt, sugar and peppercorns in a small bowl. Spread this mixture over the first fillet of fish and place the second fillet, skin side up, on top. Put a plate, the same size as the fish, on top and put a weight on the plate (3 or 4 cans of tomatoes or similar will do).

3 Refrigerate for 2 days, turning the fish about every 12 hours and basting with any juices which have come out of the fish.

4 Remove the salmon from the brine and slice thinly with a serrated knife, without slicing the skin, as you would smoked salmon.

5 Cut the brown bread into triangles and serve with the salmon. Garnish with lemon slices and sprigs of fresh dill.

COOK'S TIP

You can brush the marinade off the salmon before slicing, but the line of green along the edge of the salmon is quite attractive and, of course, full of flavour.

Thai Crab Omelette

Serves 4

INGREDIENTS

225 g/8 oz white crab meat, fresh
   or defrosted if frozen
3 spring onions, finely chopped
1 tbsp chopped fresh coriander
1 tbsp chopped fresh chives
pinch of cayenne pepper
2 tbsp vegetable oil

2 garlic cloves, crushed
1 tsp grated fresh root ginger
1 red chilli, deseeded and
   finely chopped
2 tbsp lime juice
2 lime leaves, shredded
2 tsp sugar

2 tsp Thai fish sauce
3 eggs
4 tbsp coconut cream
1 tsp salt
shredded spring onion, to garnish

1 Put the crab meat into a bowl. Check for any pieces of shell. Add the spring onions, coriander, chives and cayenne.

2 Heat 1 tablespoon of the vegetable oil and add the garlic, ginger and chilli and stir-fry for 30 seconds. Add the lime juice, lime leaves, sugar and fish sauce. Simmer for 3–4 minutes until reduced. Remove from the heat and allow to cool. Add to the crab mixture, mix well and set aside.

3 Lightly beat the eggs with the coconut cream and salt. In a frying pan, heat the remaining vegetable oil over a medium heat. Add the egg mixture and as it sets on the bottom, carefully pull the edges in towards the centre, allowing the unset egg to run underneath.

4 When the egg is nearly set, spoon the crab mixture down the centre. Cook a further 1–2 minutes to finish cooking the egg, then turn the omelette out of

the pan on to a serving dish. Allow to cool, then chill for 2–3 hours or overnight. Cut into 4 pieces and garnish with shredded spring onion.

COOK'S TIP

You can also serve this omelette warm. After adding the crab, cook for 3–4 minutes to allow the mixture to heat through, then serve immediately.

Soups & Stews

Using seafood in soups and stews makes wonderful sense. It doesn't require much cooking, making it ideal as a basis for a mid-week supper, and it combines well with an enormous variety of flavours.

It seems that only in the English-speaking world fish is undervalued. Other parts of the world use fish as a staple part of their diet and this chapter includes many dishes from a variety of places.

Don't worry though, most of the more unusual ingredients are readily available nowadays from larger supermarkets or from specialist shops. Soups such as Thai Fish Soup, Malaysian Seafood Laksa and Chinese Crab & Sweetcorn Soup illustrate the diversity of the recipes. Some of the soups are very subtly flavoured and ideal as a first course at a dinner party, such as the Creamy Scallop Soup.

Others are much more substantial and could easily be served as a main course, like the Cullen Skink. There are lots of stews and curries to choose from as well, from Red Prawn Curry to Goan Fish Curry and from Cotriade to Spanish Fish Stew.

Thai Fish Soup

Serves 4

INGREDIENTS

450 ml/16 fl oz light
   chicken stock
2 lime leaves, chopped
5 cm/2 inch piece lemon
   grass, chopped
3 tbsp lemon juice
3 tbsp Thai fish sauce
2 small, hot green chillies,
   deseeded and finely chopped

½ tsp sugar
8 small shiitake mushrooms or
   8 straw mushrooms, halved
450 g/1 lb raw prawns, peeled if
   necessary and de-veined
spring onions, to garnish

TOM YAM SAUCE
4 tbsp vegetable oil
5 garlic cloves, finely chopped
1 large shallot, finely chopped
2 large hot dried red chillies,
   roughly chopped
1 tbsp dried shrimp (optional)
1 tbsp Thai fish sauce
2 tsp sugar

1 First make the sauce. Heat the oil in a small pan and add the garlic. Cook for a few seconds until it just browns. Remove with a slotted spoon and set aside. Add the shallot to the same oil and fry until browned and crisp. Remove with a slotted spoon and set aside. Add the chillies and fry until they darken. Remove from the oil and drain on kitchen paper. Remove the pan from the heat and reserve the oil.

2 In a small food processor or spice grinder, grind the dried shrimp, if using, then add the reserved chillies, garlic and shallots. Grind together to a smooth paste. Return the pan with the original oil to a low heat, add the paste and warm. Add the Thai fish sauce and sugar and mix. Remove from the heat.

3 In a large saucepan, heat together the stock and 2 tablespoons of the tom yam

sauce. Add the lime leaves, lemon juice, lemon grass, Thai fish sauce, chillies and sugar. Simmer gently for 2 minutes.

4 Add the mushrooms and prawns and cook for a further 2–3 minutes until the prawns are cooked. Ladle in to warm bowls and serve immediately, garnished with spring onions.

Cullen Skink

Serves 4

INGREDIENTS

225 g/8 oz undyed smoked
   haddock fillet
2 tbsp butter
1 onion, finely chopped
600 ml/1 pint milk
350 g/12 oz potatoes, cut
   into cubes

350 g/12 oz cod, boned, skinned
   and cubed
150 ml/5 fl oz double cream
2 tbsp chopped fresh parsley
lemon juice, to taste
salt and pepper

TO GARNISH
lemon slices
parsley sprigs

1 Put the haddock fillet in a large frying pan and cover with boiling water. Leave for 10 minutes. Drain, reserving 300 ml/10 fl oz of the soaking water. Flake the fish, taking care to remove all the bones.

2 Heat the butter in a large saucepan and add the onion. Cook gently for 10 minutes until softened. Add the milk and bring to a gentle simmer before adding the potatoes. Cook for 10 minutes.

3 Add the reserved flaked haddock and the cod. Simmer a further 10 minutes until the cod is tender.

4 Remove about one-third of the fish and potatoes, put in a food processor and process until smooth. Alternatively, push through a sieve into a bowl. Return to the soup, together with the cream and parsley. Season to taste with salt and pepper. Taste and add a little lemon juice, if liked. Add a little of the reserved soaking water if

the soup seems to be too thick. Reheat gently and serve, garnished with lemon slices and parsley.

COOK'S TIP

Look for Finnan haddock, if you can find it. Do not use yellow dyed haddock fillet, which is often actually whiting and not haddock at all.

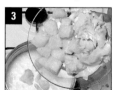

New England Clam Chowder

Serves 4

INGREDIENTS

900 g/2 lb live clams

4 rashers rindless streaky
  bacon, chopped

2 tbsp butter

1 onion, chopped

1 tbsp chopped fresh thyme

1 large potato, diced

300 ml/10 fl oz milk

1 bay leaf

150 ml/5 fl oz double cream

1 tbsp chopped fresh parsley

salt and pepper

reserve 8 clams in their shells, to
  garnish (see Cook's Tip)

1 Scrub the clams and put them into a large saucepan with a splash of water. Cook over a high heat for 3–4 minutes until all the clams have opened. Discard any that remain closed. Strain the clams, reserving the cooking liquid. Set aside until cool enough to handle.

2 Remove the clams from their shells, roughly chop if large, and set aside.

3 In a clean saucepan, fry the bacon until browned and crisp. Drain on kitchen paper. Add the butter to the same pan and when it has melted, add the onion. Cook for 4–5 minutes until softened, but not coloured. Add the thyme and cook briefly before adding the diced potato, reserved clam cooking liquid, milk and bay leaf. Bring to the boil and simmer for 10 minutes until the potato is tender, but not falling apart.

4 Transfer to a food processor and process until smooth or push through a sieve into a bowl.

5 Add the reserved clams, bacon and the cream. Simmer gently for a further 2–3 minutes until heated through. Season to taste with salt and pepper. Stir in the chopped parsley and serve.

COOK'S TIP

For a smart presentation, reserve 8 clams in their shells. Sit 2 on top of each bowl of soup to garnish.

Malaysian Seafood Laksa

Serves 4

INGREDIENTS

1 small squid, about 115 g/4 oz cleaned weight	LAKSA SPICE PASTE	TO GARNISH
4 tbsp vegetable oil	3 large dried red chillies	55 g/2 oz cucumber, cut into matchsticks
900 ml/1½ pints light chicken stock	25 g/1 oz dried shrimp (optional)	1 tbsp chopped fresh coriander
225 g/8 oz medium egg noodles	2 lemon grass stalks, chopped	1 tbsp chopped fresh mint
115 g/4 oz beansprouts	25 g/1 oz macadamia nuts	4 spring onions, thinly sliced
400 ml/14 fl oz can coconut milk	2 garlic cloves, chopped	1 red chilli, sliced into rings
8 raw tiger prawns, peeled and de-veined	2 tsp chopped fresh root ginger	1 lime, quartered
2 tsp muscovado sugar	1 tsp ground turmeric	
1 tsp salt	1 small onion, chopped	
	1 tsp ground coriander	
	3 tbsp water	

1 For the spice paste, soak the chillies in boiling water for 10 minutes until softened. Drain and deseed if you prefer. Process with the remaining spice paste ingredients in a food processor until smooth and then set aside.

2 Split the squid down one side and open out

flat. Lightly score the underside of the flesh in a criss-cross pattern and cut into 2.5 cm/1 inch squares .

3 Heat the vegetable oil in a large saucepan and fry the spice paste gently for 5–6 minutes until fragrant. Add the stock, bring to the boil, cover and simmer gently for 20 minutes.

4 Cook the egg noodles according to the packet instructions, drain and set aside. Blanch the beansprouts for 1 minute and refresh under cold water. Drain and set aside with the noodles.

5 Add the coconut milk to the stock and simmer for 3 minutes. Add the prawns, squid, sugar and salt and simmer for 4 minutes until the seafood is tender.

6 Divide the noodles and beansprouts between 4 warmed soup bowls. Spoon the hot soup over this mixture and garnish.

Chinese Crab & Sweetcorn Soup

Serves 4

INGREDIENTS

1 tbsp vegetable oil
1 small onion, finely chopped
1 garlic clove, finely chopped
1 tsp grated fresh root ginger
1 small red chilli, deseeded and
    finely chopped

2 tbsp dry sherry or Chinese
    rice wine
225 g/8 oz fresh white crab meat
325 g/11½ oz can
    sweetcorn, drained
600 ml/1 pint light chicken stock

1 tbsp light soy sauce
2 tbsp chopped fresh coriander
2 eggs, lightly beaten
salt and pepper
chilli flowers, to garnish

1 Heat the oil in a large saucepan and add the onion. Cook over a low heat, stirring occasionally, for about 5 minutes until softened. Add the garlic, ginger and chilli and cook for a further minute.

2 Add the sherry or rice wine and cook over a medium heat until reduced by about half. Add the crab meat, sweetcorn, chicken stock and soy sauce. Bring to the boil and simmer gently

for 5 minutes. Stir in the coriander. Season to taste with salt and pepper.

3 Remove the pan from the heat and pour in the eggs. Wait for a few seconds and then stir well to break the eggs into ribbons. Serve immediately, garnished with chilli flowers.

COOK'S TIP

For convenience, you could use canned crab meat. Make sure it is well drained before adding it to the soup.

Creamy Scallop Soup

Serves 4

INGREDIENTS

4 tbsp butter	350 g/12 oz prepared scallops, including corals if available	6 tbsp double cream
1 onion, finely chopped		salt and pepper
450 g/1 lb potatoes, diced	300 ml/10 fl oz milk	1 tbsp chopped fresh parsley, to garnish
600 ml/1 pint hot fish stock	2 egg yolks	

1 Melt the butter in a large saucepan over a gentle heat. Add the onion and cook very gently for 10 minutes until softened, but not coloured. Add the potatoes, season to taste with salt and pepper, cover and cook over a very low heat for a further 10 minutes.

2 Pour in the hot fish stock, bring to the boil and simmer for a further 10–15 minutes until the potatoes are tender.

3 Meanwhile, prepare the scallops. If the corals are available, roughly chop and set aside. Roughly chop the white meat and put it in a second saucepan with the milk. Bring to a gentle simmer and cook for about 6–8 minutes until the scallops are just tender.

4 When the potatoes are cooked, transfer them and their cooking liquid to a food processor or blender and process to a purée. Alternatively, press through a nylon sieve with the back of a wooden spoon. Return the mixture to a clean saucepan and add the scallops and their milk and the pieces of coral, if using.

5 Whisk together the egg yolks and cream and add to the soup, off the heat. Return the soup to a very gentle heat and, stirring constantly, reheat the soup until it thickens slightly. Do not boil or the soup will curdle. Serve immediately, sprinkled with fresh parsley.

COOK'S TIP

The soup can be made in advance up to the point where the cream and eggs are added, just before serving.

Curried Mussel Soup

Serves 4

INGREDIENTS

½ tsp coriander seeds	1 garlic clove, finely chopped	2 tbsp flour
½ tsp cumin seeds	1 tsp grated fresh root ginger	salt and pepper
900 g/2 lb live mussels	1 tsp ground turmeric	2 tbsp chopped fresh coriander,
100 ml/3½ fl oz white wine	pinch of cayenne pepper	to garnish
6 tbsp butter	600 ml/1 pint fish stock	
1 onion, finely chopped	4 tbsp double cream	

---

1 Fry the coriander and cumin seeds in a dry frying pan until they begin to smell aromatic and start to pop. Grind to a powder with a pestle and mortar. Set aside.

2 Clean the mussels by scrubbing or scraping the shells and pulling off any beards that are attached to them. Discard any with broken shells or any that do not close when tapped. Put the mussels into a large pan with the wine and cook, covered, over a high heat for 3–4 minutes, shaking the pan occasionally, until all the mussels have opened. Discard any mussels that remain closed. Drain, reserving the cooking liquid, and set aside until the mussels are cool enough to handle. Remove about two-thirds of the mussels from their shells and set them all aside. Strain the mussel cooking liquid through a fine sieve lined with muslin.

3 Heat 2 tablespoons of the butter in a large saucepan and add the onion. Fry gently for 4–5 minutes until softened, but not coloured. Add the garlic and ginger and cook for a further minute before adding the roasted and ground spices, the turmeric and cayenne. Fry for 1 minute before adding the fish stock, reserved mussel cooking liquid and cream. Simmer for 10 minutes.

4 Cream together the remaining butter and flour to a thick paste. Add the paste to the simmering soup and stir until incorporated and the soup has thickened slightly. Add the mussels and warm for 2 minutes. Garnish with coriander and serve.

Clam & Sorrel Soup

Serves 4

INGREDIENTS

900 g/2 lb live clams, scrubbed	2 shallots, finely diced	pepper
1 onion, finely chopped	1 celery stick, finely diced	dill, to garnish
150 ml/5 fl oz dry white wine	2 bay leaves	crusty bread, to serve
4 tbsp butter	150 ml/ 5 fl oz double cream	
1 small carrot, finely diced	25 g/1 oz sorrel, shredded	

1 Put the clams into a large saucepan with the onion and wine. Cover and cook over a high heat, shaking the pan occasionally, for 3–4 minutes until the clams have opened. Strain, reserving the cooking liquid, but discarding the onion. Set the clams aside until they are cool enough to handle. Strain the cooking liquid through a fine sieve lined with muslin.

2 In a clean saucepan, melt the butter over a low heat. Add the carrot, shallots and celery and cook over a low heat, stirring occasionally, for 10 minutes until softened, but not coloured. Add the reserved cooking liquid and bay leaves and simmer for a further 10 minutes.

3 Meanwhile, roughly chop the clams, if large. Add to the soup with the cream and sorrel. Simmer for 2–3 minutes until the sorrel has wilted. Season with pepper to taste and serve, garnished with dill and with plenty of crusty bread.

COOK'S TIP

Sorrel is a herb with a slightly sour, lemony flavour that goes very well with fish. It is increasingly easy to find in larger supermarkets, but is also incredibly easy to grow, as a plant.

Basque Tuna Stew

Serves 4

INGREDIENTS

5 tbsp olive oil
1 large onion, chopped
2 garlic cloves, chopped
200 g/7 oz can
    chopped tomatoes

700 g/1 lb 9 oz potatoes, cut into
    5 cm/2 inch chunks
3 green peppers, deseeded and
    roughly chopped
300 ml/10 fl oz cold water

900 g/2 lb fresh tuna, cut
    into chunks
4 slices crusty white bread
salt and pepper

1 Heat 2 tablespoons of the olive oil in a saucepan and add the onion. Cook over a medium heat, stirring occasionally, for about 8–10 minutes until soft and brown. Add the garlic and cook for a further minute. Add the tomatoes, cover and simmer over a low heat for 30 minutes until the mixture has thickened.

2 Meanwhile, in a clean saucepan, mix together the potatoes and peppers. Add the water (which should just cover the vegetables). Bring to the boil, lower the heat and simmer for about 15 minutes until the potatoes are almost tender.

3 Add the tuna and the tomato mixture to the potatoes and peppers and season to taste with salt and pepper. Cover and simmer for 6–8 minutes until the tuna is tender.

4 Meanwhile, heat the remaining oil in a large frying pan over a medium heat and add the bread slices. Fry on both sides until golden. Drain on kitchen paper. Serve with the stew.

VARIATION

Substitute any very firm-fleshed fish, such as shark or swordfish, for the tuna used in this recipe.

Goan Fish Curry

Serves 4

INGREDIENTS

750 g/1 lb 10 oz monkfish fillet, cut into chunks
1 tbsp cider vinegar
1 tsp salt
1 tsp ground turmeric
3 tbsp vegetable oil

2 garlic cloves, crushed
1 small onion, finely chopped
2 tsp ground coriander
1 tsp cayenne pepper
2 tsp paprika

2 tbsp tamarind pulp plus 2 tbsp boiling water (see method)
85 g/3 oz creamed coconut, cut into pieces
300 ml/10 fl oz warm water
plain boiled rice, to serve

1 Put the fish on a plate and drizzle over the vinegar. Mix together half the salt and half the turmeric and sprinkle evenly over the fish. Cover and set aside for 20 minutes.

2 Heat the oil in a frying pan and add the garlic. Brown slightly, then add the onion and fry over a low heat for 3–4 minutes until soft, but not browned. Add the ground coriander and stir for 1 minute.

3 Mix the remaining turmeric, the cayenne and paprika with about 2 tablespoons water to make a paste. Add this to the pan with the remaining salt and cook over a low heat for 1–2 minutes.

4 In a small bowl, mix the tamarind pulp with the 2 tablespoons boiling water and stir well. When the water appears thick and the pulp has come away from the seeds, pass this mixture through a sieve, rubbing the pulp thoroughly. Discard the seeds once finished.

5 Add the creamed coconut, warm water and tamarind paste to the pan and stir until the coconut has dissolved. Add the pieces of fish and any juices remaining on the plate and simmer over a low heat for 4–5 minutes until the sauce has thickened and the fish is just tender. Serve immediately on a bed of plain boiled rice.

Thai Green Fish Curry

Serves 4

INGREDIENTS

2 tbsp vegetable oil
1 garlic clove, chopped
1 small aubergine, diced
125 ml/4 fl oz coconut cream
2 tbsp Thai fish sauce
1 tsp sugar
225 g/8 oz firm white fish, cut
    into pieces, such as cod,
    haddock, halibut
125 ml/4 fl oz fish stock
2 lime leaves, finely shredded

about 15 leaves Thai basil, if
    available, or ordinary basil
plain boiled rice or noodles,
    to serve

GREEN CURRY PASTE
5 fresh green chillies, deseeded
    and chopped
2 tsp chopped lemon grass
1 large shallot, chopped
2 garlic cloves, chopped

1 tsp grated fresh root ginger or
    galangal, if available
2 coriander roots, chopped
½ tsp ground coriander
¼ tsp ground cumin
1 kaffir lime leaf, finely chopped
1 tsp shrimp paste (optional)
½ tsp salt

1 Make the curry paste. Put all the ingredients into a blender or spice grinder and blend to a smooth paste, adding a little water if necessary. Alternatively, pound the ingredients, using a mortar and pestle, until smooth. Set aside.

2 In a frying pan or wok, heat the oil until almost smoking and add the garlic. Stir-fry over a medium heat until golden. Add the curry paste and stir-fry for a few seconds before adding the aubergine. Stir-fry for about 4–5 minutes until softened.

3 Add the coconut cream. Bring the mixture to the boil and stir until the coconut cream thickens and curdles slightly. Add the Thai fish sauce and sugar to the frying pan or wok and stir well into the mixture.

4 Add the fish pieces and fish stock. Simmer for 3–4 minutes, stirring occasionally, until the fish is just tender. Add the lime leaves and basil, and then cook for a further minute. Remove from the frying pan and serve with plain boiled rice or noodles.

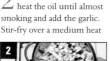

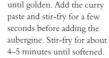

Mackerel Escabeche

Serves 4

INGREDIENTS

150 ml/5 fl oz olive oil

4 mackerel, filleted

2 tbsp seasoned flour,
   for dusting

4 tbsp red wine vinegar

1 onion, thinly sliced

1 strip orange rind, removed
   with a potato peeler

1 fresh thyme sprig

1 fresh rosemary sprig

1 fresh bay leaf

4 garlic cloves, crushed

2 fresh red chillies, bruised

1 tsp salt

3 tbsp chopped fresh
   flat-leaved parsley

crusty bread, to serve

1 Heat half the olive oil in a large frying pan and dust the mackerel fillets with the seasoned flour.

2 Add the fish to the frying pan, in batches if necessary, and cook for about 30 seconds on each side until not quite cooked through.

3 Using a fish slice, carefully transfer the mackerel to a shallow dish, large enough to hold the fillets in a single layer.

4 Add the the vinegar, onion, orange rind, thyme, rosemary, bay leaf, garlic, chillies and salt to the pan. Simmer over a low heat for 10 minutes.

5 Add the remaining olive oil and the chopped parsley. Pour the mixture over the fish and set aside until cold. Serve with plenty of crusty bread.

VARIATION

Substitute 12 whole sardines, cleaned and with their heads removed. Cook in the same way. Tuna steaks are also very delicious served escabeche.

Lemon Sole in a Sweet & Sour Sauce

Serves 4

INGREDIENTS

2 large lemon sole, filleted	115 g/4 oz hazelnuts, chopped	2 tbsp red wine vinegar
flour, for dredging	50 g/1¾ oz pine kernels	150 ml/5 fl oz water
2 tbsp olive oil, plus extra	50 g/1¾ oz raisins	3 tbsp chopped fresh parsley
for frying	225 g/8 oz ripe tomatoes, peeled	salt and pepper
2 onions, thinly sliced	and chopped	boiled new potatoes, to serve

1 Wash and dry the fish fillets. Dredge lightly with flour. In a large frying pan, heat about 2.5 cm/ 1 inch of olive oil – enough just to cover the fish – over a medium-high heat. Add the fish fillets, 2 at a time, and completely submerge in the oil. Cook for 5–6 minutes, then drain on kitchen paper. Set aside. Fry the remaining fish in the same way.

2 Heat the remaining 2 tablespoons of olive oil in a large saucepan. Add the onions and cook for 7–8 minutes until soft and starting to brown. Add the hazelnuts, pine kernels and raisins and fry for a further 1–2 minutes until the nuts are golden. Add the tomatoes and cook for 5 minutes until just softened.

3 Add the vinegar and simmer over a low heat for 5 minutes. Add the water and parsley, season to taste with salt and pepper and stir well. Simmer gently for a further 5 minutes.

4 Lower the fried fish into the sauce and simmer gently for 10 minutes. Serve with boiled new potatoes.

COOK'S TIP

In the Middle East, many different types of fish are treated this way, but a particular favourite is red mullet. Small fish can be left whole (after cleaning and scaling).

Haddock Baked in Yogurt

Serves 4

INGREDIENTS

2 large onions, thinly sliced
900 g/2 lb haddock fillet, from
  the head end
425 ml/15 fl oz natural yogurt
2 tbsp lemon juice
1 tsp sugar

2 tsp ground cumin
2 tsp ground coriander
pinch of garam masala
pinch of cayenne pepper
1 tsp grated fresh root ginger
3 tbsp vegetable oil

4 tbsp cold unsalted butter, cut
  into pieces
salt and pepper

1 Line a large ovenproof dish with the onion slices. Cut the fish into strips widthways and lay the strips in a single layer on top of the onion slices.

2 In a bowl, mix together the yogurt, lemon juice, sugar, cumin, coriander, garam masala, cayenne, ginger, oil and seasoning. Pour this sauce over the fish, making sure it goes under the fish as well. Cover tightly.

3 Bake in a preheated oven, 190°C/375°F/Gas Mark 5 for 30 minutes or until the fish is just tender and flakes easily.

4 Carefully pour the sauce off the fish into a small saucepan. Keep the fish warm. Bring the sauce to the boil, lower the heat and simmer gently to reduce the sauce to about 350 ml/ 12 fl oz. Remove the pan from the heat.

5 Add the cubes of butter to the sauce and whisk until melted and fully incorporated. Pour the sauce back over the fish and serve.

COOK'S TIP

When you pour the sauce off the fish it will look thin and separated, but reducing and stirring in the butter will help to amalgamate it.

Cod Italienne

Serves 4

INGREDIENTS

2 tbsp olive oil
1 onion, finely chopped
2 garlic cloves, finely chopped
2 tsp chopped fresh thyme
150 ml/5 fl oz red wine
2 x 400 g/14 oz cans
   chopped tomatoes
pinch of sugar

50 g/1¾ oz stoned black olives,
   roughly chopped
50 g/1¾ oz stoned green olives,
   roughly chopped
2 tbsp capers, drained, rinsed
   and roughly chopped
2 tbsp chopped fresh basil

4 cod steaks, each weighing
   about 175 g/6 oz
150 g/5½ oz ball buffalo
   mozzarella, drained
   and sliced
salt and pepper
buttered noodles, to serve

1 Heat the olive oil in a large saucepan. Add the onion and fry over a low heat for 5 minutes until softened, but not coloured. Add the garlic and thyme and cook for a further minute.

2 Increase the heat and add the wine. Simmer until reduced and syrupy. Add the tomatoes and sugar and bring to the boil. Cover and simmer for 30 minutes. Uncover and simmer for a further 20 minutes until

thick. Stir in the olives, capers and basil. Season to taste.

3 Arrange the cod steaks in a shallow ovenproof dish (a lasagne dish is perfect) and spoon the tomato sauce over the top. Bake in a preheated oven, 190°C/375°F/Gas Mark 5 for 20–25 minutes, until the fish is just tender.

4 Remove the dish from the oven and arrange the mozzarella slices on top of the fish.

5 Return to the oven for a further 5–10 minutes until the cheese has melted. Serve immediately with buttered noodles.

VARIATION

Other white fish steaks would work equally well and, if you want to push the boat out, try turbot.

Cod Curry

Serves 4

INGREDIENTS

1 tbsp vegetable oil
1 small onion, chopped
2 garlic cloves, chopped
2.5 cm/1 in piece fresh root
   ginger, roughly chopped
2 large ripe tomatoes, peeled and
   roughly chopped

150 ml/5 fl oz fish stock
1 tbsp medium curry paste
1 tsp ground coriander
400 g/14 oz can chickpeas,
   drained and rinsed
750 g/1 lb 10 oz cod fillet, cut
   into large chunks

4 tbsp chopped fresh coriander
4 tbsp thick yogurt
salt and pepper
steamed basmati rice, to serve

1 Heat the oil in a large saucepan and add the onion, garlic and ginger. Fry over a low heat, stirring occasionally, for 4–5 minutes until softened. Remove from the heat. Put the onion mixture into a food processor or blender with the tomatoes and fish stock and process until smooth.

2 Return the mixture to the saucepan and add the curry paste, ground coriander and chickpeas. Mix together well, then simmer gently for 15 minutes until thickened.

3 Add the pieces of fish and return to a simmer. Cook for 5 minutes until the fish is just tender. Remove from the heat and leave to stand for 2–3 minutes.

4 Stir in the coriander and yogurt. Season and serve with steamed basmati rice.

VARIATION

Instead of cod, make this curry using raw prawns and omit the chickpeas.

Home-salted Cod with Chickpeas

Serves 6

INGREDIENTS

50 g/1¾ oz sea salt
1.5 kg/3 lb 5oz fresh cod fillet,
    from the head end, skin on
225 g/8 oz dried chickpeas,
    soaked overnight
1 fresh red chilli

4 garlic cloves
2 bay leaves
1 tbsp olive oil
300 ml/10 fl oz chicken stock
extra-virgin olive oil, for drizzling
pepper

GREMOLATA
3 tbsp chopped fresh parsley
2 garlic cloves, finely chopped
finely grated rind of 1 lemon

1 Sprinkle the salt over both sides of the cod fillet. Place in a shallow dish, cover with clingfilm and refrigerate for 48 hours. When you are ready to cook, remove the cod from the refrigerator and rinse under cold water. Leave to soak in cold water for 2 hours.

2 Drain the chickpeas, rinse them thoroughly and drain again. Put into a large saucepan. Add double their volume of water and bring to the boil over a low heat. Remove any scum that rises to the surface. Split the chilli lengthways and add it to the chickpeas together with the whole garlic cloves and the bay leaves. Cover and simmer for 1½–2 hours until the chickpeas are very tender, skimming the surface occasionally if necessary.

3 Drain the cod and pat dry with kitchen paper. Brush with the olive oil and season well with pepper (but no salt). Cook under a preheated grill or on a hot ridged grill pan for about 3–4 minutes on each side until tender. Meanwhile, add the chicken stock to the chickpeas and bring back to the boil. Keep warm.

4 For the gremolata, mix together the parsley, garlic and finely grated lemon rind.

5 To serve, ladle the chickpeas and their cooking liquid into 6 warmed soup bowls. Top with the grilled cod and sprinkle over the gremolata. Drizzle generously with olive oil and serve immediately.

Cotriade

Serves 6

INGREDIENTS

large pinch saffron
600 ml/1 pint hot fish stock
1 tbsp olive oil
2 tbsp butter
1 onion, sliced
2 garlic cloves, chopped
1 leek, sliced
1 small fennel bulb, thinly sliced

450 g/1 lb potatoes, cut
    into chunks
150 ml/5 fl oz dry white wine
1 tbsp fresh thyme leaves
2 bay leaves
4 ripe tomatoes, peeled
    and chopped

900 g/2 lb mixed fish, such as
    haddock, hake, mackerel,
    red or grey mullet,
    roughly chopped
2 tbsp chopped fresh parsley
salt and pepper
crusty bread, to serve

1 Using a mortar and pestle, crush the saffron and add to the fish stock. Stir and leave to infuse for at least 10 minutes.

2 In a large saucepan, heat the oil and butter. Add the onion and cook over a low heat, stirring frequently, for 4–5 minutes until softened. Add the garlic, leek, fennel and potatoes. Cover and cook for a further 10–15 minutes until the vegetables are softened.

3 Add the wine and boil rapidly for 3–4 minutes until reduced by half. Add the thyme, bay leaves and tomatoes and stir well. Add the saffron-infused fish stock. Bring to the boil, cover and simmer over a low heat for 15 minutes until the vegetables are tender.

4 Add the fish, return to the boil and simmer for a further 3–4 minutes until all the fish is tender. Add the parsley and season to taste.

Using a perforated spoon, remove the fish and vegetables to a warmed serving dish. Serve the soup with plenty of crusty bread.

VARIATION

Once the fish and vegetables have been cooked, the soup could be blended and passed through a sieve to give a smooth fish soup.

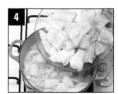

Squid Stew

Serves 4

INGREDIENTS

750 g/1 lb 10 oz squid
3 tbsp olive oil
1 onion, chopped
3 garlic cloves, finely chopped

1 tsp fresh thyme leaves
400 g/14 oz can chopped
 tomatoes
150 ml/5 fl oz red wine

300 ml/10 fl oz water
1 tbsp chopped fresh parsley
salt and pepper

1 To prepare whole squid, hold the body firmly and grasp the tentacles just inside the body. Pull firmly to remove the innards. Find the transparent quill and remove. Grasp the wings on the outside of the body and pull to remove the outer skin. Trim the tentacles just below the beak and reserve. Wash the body and tentacles under running water. Slice the body into rings. Drain well on kitchen paper.

2 Heat the oil in a large, flameproof casserole. Add the prepared squid and cook over a medium heat, stirring occasionally, until lightly browned.

3 Reduce the heat and add the onion, garlic and thyme. Cook, stirring occasionally, for a further 5 minutes until softened.

4 Stir in the tomatoes, red wine and water. Bring to the boil, then transfer the casserole to a preheated oven, 140°C/ 275°F/Gas Mark 1 for 2 hours. Stir in the parsley and season to taste with salt and pepper and serve.

VARIATION

This stew can be used as the basis for a more substantial fish stew. Before adding the parsley, add extra seafood, such as scallops, pieces of fish fillet, large prawns or even cooked lobster. Return the stew to the boil and cook for a further 2 minutes. Add the parsley and season to taste.

Spanish Fish Stew

Serves 6

INGREDIENTS

5 tbsp olive oil	3 garlic cloves, roughly chopped	6 langoustines
2 large onions, finely chopped	350 g/12 oz cooked lobster	18 live mussels, scrubbed,
2 ripe tomatoes, peeled, deseeded	200 g/7 oz cleaned squid	beards removed
and diced	200 g/7 oz monkfish fillet	8 large live clams, scrubbed
2 slices white bread,	200 g/7 oz cod fillet, skinned	1 tbsp chopped fresh parsley
crusts removed	1 tbsp plain flour	125 ml/4 fl oz brandy
4 almonds, toasted	6 large raw prawns	salt and pepper

1 Heat 3 tablespoons of the oil in a frying pan, add the onions and cook gently for 10–15 minutes until lightly golden, adding a little water to prevent them from sticking, if necessary. Add the tomatoes and cook until they have disintegrated and the oil has separated away from them.

2 Heat 1 tablespoon of the remaining oil and fry the slices of bread until crisp. Break into rough pieces and put into a mortar with the almonds and 2 garlic cloves.

Pound to make a fine paste. Alternatively, blend to a paste in a food processor.

3 To prepare the lobster, split it lengthways. Remove and discard the intestinal vein which runs down the tail, the stomach sac and the spongy-looking gills. Crack the claws and remove the meat. Take out the flesh from the tail and chop into large chunks. Slice the squid into rings.

4 Season the monkfish, cod and lobster and dust

with a little flour. In a frying pan, heat the remaining oil and brown the fish, lobster, prawns and langoustines separately: Arrange them in a flameproof casserole as they turn brown.

5 Add the mussels and clams to the casserole. Add the remaining garlic and parsley and place the casserole over a low heat. Pour in the brandy and ignite. When the flames have died down, add the tomato mixture and just enough water to cover. Bring to the boil and simmer for 3–4 minutes until the shellfish have opened. Discard any that remain closed. Stir in the bread mixture and season to taste. Simmer a further 5 minutes until the fish is tender.

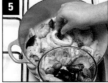

Moroccan Fish Tagine

Serves 4

INGREDIENTS

2 tbsp olive oil	½ tsp ground turmeric	50 g/1¾ oz stoned green olives
1 large onion, finely chopped	200 g/7 oz can chopped tomatoes	1 tbsp chopped preserved lemon
large pinch saffron strands	300 ml/10 fl oz fish stock	3 tbsp chopped fresh coriander
½ tsp ground cinnamon	4 small red mullet cleaned, boned	salt and pepper
1 tsp ground coriander	and heads and tails removed	couscous, to serve
½ tsp ground cumin		

1 Heat the olive oil in a large saucepan or flameproof casserole. Add the onion and cook over a low heat, stirring occasionally, for 10 minutes until softened, but not coloured. Add the saffron, cinnamon, ground coriander, cumin and turmeric and cook, stirring constantly, for a further 30 seconds.

2 Add the chopped tomatoes and fish stock and stir well. Bring to the boil, cover and simmer for 15 minutes. Uncover the casserole and simmer for a further 20–35 minutes until the sauce has thickened.

3 Cut each red mullet in half then add the pieces to the pan, pushing them into the sauce. Simmer gently for a further 5–6 minutes until the fish is just cooked.

4 Carefully stir in the olives, preserved lemon and the chopped fresh coriander. Season to taste with salt and pepper and serve straight from the casserole with couscous.

COOK'S TIP

Preserved lemons are simple to make yourself. Take enough lemons to fill a preserving jar completely and quarter them lengthways without cutting all the way through. Pack the lemons with 4 tablespoons sea salt per lemon. Add the juice of an additional lemon and top up with water to cover. Leave for at least 1 month before using.

Stewed Sardines

Serves 4

INGREDIENTS

50 g/1¾ oz raisins

3 tbsp Marsala

4 tbsp olive oil

225 g/8 oz baby onions, halved
    if large

2 garlic cloves, chopped

1 tbsp chopped fresh sage

4 large tomatoes, peeled
    and chopped

150 ml/5 fl oz fish or
    vegetable stock

2 tbsp balsamic vinegar

450 g/1 lb fresh sardines, cleaned

4 tbsp stoned black olives

4 tbsp pine kernels, toasted

2 tbsp chopped fresh parsley

1 Put the raisins in a small bowl and pour over the Marsala. Leave to soak for about 1 hour until the raisins are plump. Strain, reserving both the Marsala and the raisins.

2 Heat the olive oil in a large saucepan. Add the onions and fry over a low heat, stirring occasionally, for 15 minutes until golden and tender. Add the garlic and sage and cook for a further minute. Add the tomatoes, fry for a further 2–3 minutes, then add the stock, vinegar and reserved Marsala. Bring to the boil, cover and simmer for 25 minutes.

3 Add the sardines to the stew and simmer over a low heat for 2–3 minutes before adding the raisins, olives and pine kernels. Continue to simmer for a final 2–3 minutes until the fish are cooked through. Add the chopped parsley and serve immediately.

VARIATION

Substitute Home-salted Cod (see page 90) or smoked cod for the sardines.

Red Prawn Curry

Serves 4

INGREDIENTS

2 tbsp vegetable oil
1 garlic clove, finely chopped
200 ml/7 fl oz coconut milk
2 tbsp Thai fish sauce
1 tsp sugar
12 large raw prawns, peeled and de-veined
2 lime leaves, finely shredded

1 small red chilli, deseeded and thinly sliced
10 leaves Thai basil, if available, or ordinary basil

RED CURRY PASTE
3 dried long red chillies
½ tsp ground coriander
¼ tsp ground cumin

1 tsp ground black pepper
2 garlic cloves, chopped
2 lemon grass stalks, chopped
1 kaffir lime leaf, finely chopped
1 tsp grated fresh root ginger or galangal, if available
1 tsp shrimp paste (optional)
½ tsp salt

1 First, make the red curry paste. Put all the curry paste ingredients into a blender or spice grinder and blend to form a smooth paste, adding a little water if necessary. Alternatively, pound the ingredients using a mortar and pestle until smooth. Set aside.

2 Heat the oil in a wok or frying pan until almost smoking. Add the chopped garlic and stir-fry until golden. Stir in 1 tablespoon of the curry paste and stir-fry for a further minute. Add half the coconut milk, the Thai fish sauce and the sugar. Stir thoroughly. The mixture should thicken slightly.

3 Add the prawns and simmer over a low heat for 3–4 minutes until they change colour. Gently stir in the remaining coconut milk, the shredded lime leaves and the red chilli. Cook over a low heat for a further 2–3 minutes until the prawns are just tender.

4 Add the basil leaves, stir until wilted and serve.

COOK'S TIP

This recipe makes a little more curry paste than you need, but it keeps well. Stir a little into canned tuna with some chopped spring onion, lime juice and pinto beans for a delicious sandwich filling.

Curried Prawns with Courgettes

Serves 4

INGREDIENTS

350 g/12 oz small courgettes	5 tbsp chopped fresh coriander	200 g/7 oz can chopped
1 tsp salt	1 fresh green chilli, deseeded and	tomatoes
450 g/1 lb raw tiger prawns,	finely chopped	1 tsp grated fresh root ginger
peeled and de-veined	½ tsp ground turmeric	1 tbsp lemon juice
5 tbsp vegetable oil	1½ tsp ground cumin	lime wedges, to garnish
4 garlic cloves, finely chopped	pinch of cayenne pepper	steamed basmati rice, to serve

1 Wash and trim the courgettes. Cut into small batons. Put into a colander and sprinkle with a little of the salt. Set aside for 30 minutes. Rinse, drain and pat dry with kitchen paper. Spread the prawns on kitchen paper to drain.

2 In a wok or frying pan, heat the oil over a high heat. Add the garlic and stir-fry. As soon as the garlic begins to brown, add the courgettes, chopped coriander, green chilli, turmeric, cumin, cayenne, tomatoes, ginger, lemon juice and remaining salt. Stir well and bring to the boil.

3 Cover and simmer over a low heat for about 5 minutes. Uncover and add the prawns.

4 Increase the heat to high and simmer for about 5 minutes to reduce the liquid to a thick sauce. Serve immediately with steamed basmati rice, garnished with lime wedges.

VARIATION

If you can't find cooked tiger prawns for this recipe, use cooked peeled prawns instead but these release quite a lot of liquid so you may need to increase the final simmering time to thicken the sauce.

Salads,
Summer & Dishes
Suppers

Fish is the perfect ingredient for a mid-week supper because it cooks so quickly. It is also wonderful marinated and simply grilled or barbecued and makes a perfect ingredient in a salad, either warm or cold.

This chapter contains a variety of recipes designed to be simple, but to taste as if you have spent hours preparing them. There are substantial main course salads, such as Tuna Bean Salad, Moroccan Couscous Salad and Caesar Salad.

Quick suppers include the best Cod & Chips ever, plus Salmon Frittata and Tuna Fishcakes. Lots of barbecue ideas are here as well, including Barbecued Monkfish, Char-grilled Scallops and Mixed Seafood Brochettes.

Caesar Salad

Serves 4

INGREDIENTS

1 large cos lettuce or
   2 Little Gem lettuces
4 canned anchovies, drained and
   halved lengthways
Parmesan shavings, to garnish

DRESSING
2 garlic cloves, crushed

1½ tsp Dijon mustard
1 tsp Worcestershire sauce
4 canned anchovies, drained
   and chopped
1 egg yolk
1 tbsp lemon juice
150 ml/5 fl oz olive oil

4 tbsp freshly grated
   Parmesan cheese
salt and pepper

CROÛTONS
4 thick slices day-old bread
2 tbsp olive oil
1 garlic clove, crushed

1 Make the dressing. Put the garlic, mustard, Worcestershire sauce, anchovies, egg yolk, lemon juice and seasoning into a food processor or blender and process for 30 seconds, until foaming. With the motor running, add the olive oil, drop by drop to begin with, until the mixture begins to thicken, then in a steady stream until all the oil has been fully incorporated. Scrape the dressing into a bowl. Add a little hot water if the dressing is too thick. Stir in the grated Parmesan cheese. Taste for seasoning, cover and set aside in the refrigerator until required.

2 For the croûtons, cut the bread into 1 cm/1 inch cubes. Toss with the oil and garlic in a bowl. Transfer to a baking tray in a single layer. Bake in a preheated oven, 180°C/350°F/ Gas Mark 4, for 15–20 minutes, stirring occasionally, until the croûtons are browned and crisp. Remove from the oven and allow to cool. Set aside.

3 Separate the cos or Little Gem lettuces into individual leaves and wash. Tear into pieces and spin dry in a salad spinner. Alternatively, dry the leaves on kitchen paper. (Excess moisture will dilute the dressing and make the salad taste watery.) Transfer to a plastic bag and refrigerate until needed.

4 To assemble the salad, put the lettuce pieces into a large serving bowl. Add the dressing and toss thoroughly until all the leaves are coated. Top with the halved anchovies, croûtons and Parmesan shavings. Serve at once.

Moroccan Couscous Salad

Serves 4

INGREDIENTS

225 g/8 oz couscous
1 cinnamon stick, about 5 cm/
    2 inches long
2 tsp coriander seeds
1 tsp cumin seeds
2 tbsp olive oil
1 small onion, finely chopped

2 garlic cloves, finely chopped
½ tsp ground turmeric
pinch of cayenne pepper
1 tbsp lemon juice
4 tbsp sultanas
3 ripe plum tomatoes, chopped
85 g/3 oz cucumber, chopped

4 spring onions, sliced
200 g/7 oz can tuna in olive oil,
    drained and flaked
3 tbsp chopped fresh coriander
salt and pepper

1 Cook the couscous according to the packet instructions, omitting any butter recommended. Transfer to a large bowl and set aside.

2 Heat a small frying pan and add the cinnamon stick, coriander seeds and cumin seeds. Cook over a high heat until the seeds begin to pop and smell fragrant. Remove from the heat and pour the seeds into a mortar. Grind with a pestle to a fine powder. Alternatively, grind in a spice grinder. Set aside.

3 Heat the oil in a clean frying pan and add the onion. Cook over a low heat, stirring occasionally, for 7–8 minutes until softened and lightly browned. Add the garlic and cook for a further minute. Stir in the roasted and ground spices, the turmeric and cayenne and cook for a further minute. Remove the pan from the heat and stir in the lemon juice. Add this mixture to the couscous and mix well together, ensuring that all of the grains are coated.

4 Add the sultanas, tomatoes, cucumber, spring onions, tuna and chopped coriander. Season with salt and pepper to taste and mix together. Allow to cool completely and serve at room temperature.

Tuna Niçoise Salad

Serves 4

INGREDIENTS

4 eggs	1 garlic clove, crushed	175 g/6 oz cucumber, peeled, cut
450 g/1 lb new potatoes	1½ tsp Dijon mustard	in half and sliced
115 g/4 oz dwarf green beans,	2 tsp lemon juice	50 g/1¾ oz stoned black olives
trimmed and halved	2 tbsp chopped fresh basil	50 g/1¾ oz can anchovies in
2 x 175 g/6 oz tuna steaks	2 Little Gem lettuces	oil, drained
6 tbsp olive oil, plus extra	200 g/7 oz cherry tomatoes,	salt and pepper
for brushing	halved	

1 Bring a small saucepan of water to the boil. Add the eggs and cook for 7–9 minutes from when the water returns to the boil – 7 minutes for a slightly soft centre, 9 minutes for a firm centre. Drain and refresh under cold running water. Set aside.

2 Cook the potatoes in lightly salted boiling water for 10–12 minutes until tender. Add the beans 3 minutes before the end of the cooking time. Drain both vegetables well and refresh under cold water. Drain well again.

3 Wash the tuna steaks and pat dry with kitchen paper. Brush both sides with a little olive oil and season to taste with salt and pepper. Cook on a preheated ridged grill pan for 2–3 minutes each side, until just tender but still slightly pink in the centre. Set aside to rest.

4 Whisk together the garlic, mustard, lemon juice, basil and seasoning. Whisk in the olive oil.

5 To assemble the salad, break apart the lettuces and tear the leaves into large pieces. Divide between individual serving plates. Next, add the potatoes and beans, tomatoes, cucumber and olives. Toss lightly together. Shell the eggs and cut into quarters lengthways. Arrange these on top of the salad. Scatter the anchovies over the salad.

6 Flake the tuna steaks and arrange on the salads. Pour over the dressing and serve immediately.

VARIATION

Use 2 x 200 g/7 oz cans of tuna in olive oil, drained and flaked, instead of the fresh tuna.

Tuna Bean Salad

Serves 4

INGREDIENTS

225 g/8 oz dried haricot beans
1 tbsp lemon juice
5 tbsp extra-virgin olive oil, plus
   extra for brushing
1 garlic clove, finely chopped

1 small red onion, very thinly
   sliced (optional)
1 tbsp chopped fresh parsley
4 x 175 g/6 oz tuna steaks
salt and pepper

TO GARNISH
parsley sprigs
lemon wedges

1 Put the haricot beans in a bowl and cover with at least twice their volume of cold water. Set aside to soak for 8 hours or overnight.

2 When you are ready to cook, drain the beans and place in a saucepan with twice their volume of fresh water. Bring slowly to the boil, skimming off any scum that rises to the surface. Boil the beans vigorously for 10 minutes, then reduce the heat and simmer for a further 1¼–1½ hours until the beans are tender.

3 Meanwhile, mix together the lemon juice, olive oil and garlic and season to taste with salt and pepper. Drain the beans thoroughly and mix together with the olive oil mixture, onion, if using, and parsley. Season to taste and set aside.

4 Wash the tuna steaks and pat dry with kitchen paper. Brush both sides lightly with olive oil and season. Cook on a preheated ridged grill pan for 2 minutes on each side until just pink in the centre.

5 Divide the bean salad between 4 serving plates. Top each with a tuna steak. Garnish with parsley sprigs and lemon wedges and serve immediately while the tuna is still warm.

COOK'S TIP

You could use canned haricot beans instead of dried. Reheat according to the instructions on the can, drain and toss with the dressing as above.

Thai Seafood Salad

Serves 4

INGREDIENTS

450 g/1 lb live mussels
8 raw tiger prawns
350 g/12 oz squid, cleaned and
    sliced widthways into rings
115 g/4 oz cooked peeled prawns
½ red onion, thinly sliced
½ red pepper, deseeded and
    thinly sliced

115 g/4 oz beansprouts
115 g/4 oz shredded pak choy

DRESSING
1 garlic clove, crushed
1 red chilli, deseeded and
    finely chopped
1 tsp grated fresh root ginger

2 tbsp chopped fresh coriander
1 tbsp lime juice
1 tsp finely grated lime rind
1 tbsp light soy sauce
5 tbsp sunflower or
    groundnut oil
2 tsp sesame oil
salt and pepper

1 Prepare the mussels by scrubbing or scraping the shells and pulling off any beards. Place in a large saucepan with just the water that clings to their shells. Cook over a high heat for 3–4 minutes, shaking the pan occasionally, until all the mussels have opened. Discard any that remain closed. Drain the mussels, reserving the poaching liquid, and refresh the mussels under cold water. Drain again and set aside.

2 Bring the reserved cooking liquid to the boil and add the tiger prawns. Simmer for 5 minutes. Add the squid and cook for a further 2 minutes until cooked through. Remove the seafood with a perforated spoon and plunge into a bowl of cold water. Drain well. Reserve the cooking liquid.

3 Remove the mussels from their shells and put into a bowl with the tiger prawns, squid and cooked peeled prawns. Cover and refrigerate for 1 hour.

4 For the dressing, put all the ingredients, except the sunflower and groundnut oils, into a blender and blend to a smooth paste. Add both the oils, the reserved cooking liquid and 4 tbsp cold water. Season to taste with salt and pepper. Blend to combine.

5 Just before serving, combine the onion, red pepper, beansprouts and pak choy in a bowl and toss with 2–3 tbsp of the dressing. Arrange the vegetables on a large serving plate or in a bowl. Toss the remaining dressing with the seafood to coat and add to the vegetables. Serve at once.

Skate & Spinach Salad

Serves 4

INGREDIENTS

700 g/1 lb 9 oz skate
    wings, trimmed
2 fresh rosemary sprigs
1 fresh bay leaf
1 tbsp black peppercorns
1 lemon, quartered

450 g/1 lb baby spinach leaves
1 tbsp olive oil
1 small red onion, thinly sliced
2 garlic cloves, crushed
½ tsp chilli flakes

50 g/1¾ oz pine kernels,
    lightly toasted
50 g/1¾ oz raisins
1 tbsp light muscovado sugar
2 tbsp chopped fresh parsley

1 Put the skate wings into a large saucepan with the rosemary, bay leaf, peppercorns and lemon quarters. Cover with cold water and bring to the boil. Cover and simmer over a low heat for 4–5 minutes until the flesh begins to come away from the cartilage. Remove the pan from the heat and set aside for 15 minutes.

2 Lift the fish from the poaching water and remove the flesh from the fish in shreds. Set aside.

3 Meanwhile, place the spinach in a clean saucepan with just the water that clings to the leaves after washing. Cook over a high heat for 30 seconds until just wilted. Drain, refresh under cold water and drain well once more. Squeeze out any excess water and set aside.

4 Heat the olive oil in a large, deep frying pan. Add the red onion and fry over a low heat, stirring occasionally, for 3–4 minutes until softened, but not browned. Add the garlic,

chilli flakes, pine kernels, raisins and sugar. Cook for 1–2 minutes, then add the spinach and toss for 1 minute until heated through.

5 Gently fold in the skate and cook for a further minute. Season well with salt and pepper.

6 Divide the salad between 4 serving plates and sprinkle with the chopped parsley. Serve immediately.

Grilled Red Mullet

Serves 4

INGREDIENTS

1 lemon, thinly sliced

2 garlic cloves, crushed

4 fresh flat-leaved parsley sprigs

4 fresh thyme sprigs

8 fresh sage leaves

2 large shallots, sliced

8 small red mullet, cleaned

8 slices Parma ham

salt and pepper

SAUTE POTATOES AND SHALLOTS

4 tbsp olive oil

900 g/2 lb potatoes, diced

8 whole garlic cloves, unpeeled

12 small whole shallots

DRESSING

4 tbsp olive oil

1 tbsp lemon juice

1 tbsp chopped fresh
    flat-leaved parsley

1 tbsp chopped fresh chives

salt and pepper

1 For the sauté potatoes and shallots, heat the olive oil in a large, heavy-based frying pan and add the potatoes, garlic cloves and shallots. Cook over a low heat, stirring frequently, for 12–15 minutes until golden, crisp and tender.

2 Meanwhile, divide the lemon slices, halved if necessary, garlic, parsley, thyme, sage and shallots between the cavities of the fish. Season well with salt and pepper. Wrap a slice of Parma ham around each fish. Secure with a cocktail stick.

3 Arrange the fish on a grill pan and cook under a preheated hot grill for 5–6 minutes on each side until tender.

4 To make the dressing, whisk together the oil and lemon juice and stir in the finely chopped parsley and chives. Season to taste with salt and pepper.

5 Divide the potatoes and shallots between 4 serving plates and top each with the fish. Drizzle the dressing around the fish and serve immediately.

Poached Rainbow Trout

Serves 4

INGREDIENTS

4 x 375 g/12 oz rainbow
    trout, cleaned
700 g/1 lb 9 oz new potatoes
3 spring onions, finely chopped
1 egg, hard-boiled and chopped

WATERCRESS MAYONNAISE
1 egg yolk
1 tsp Dijon mustard
50 g/2 oz watercress leaves,
    chopped

1 tsp white wine vinegar
225 ml/8 fl oz light olive oil
salt and pepper

COURT-BOUILLON
850 ml/1½ pints cold water
850 ml/1½ pints dry white wine
3 tbsp white wine vinegar
2 large carrots, roughly chopped
1 onion, roughly chopped
2 celery sticks, roughly chopped

2 leeks, roughly chopped
2 garlic cloves, roughly chopped
2 fresh bay leaves
4 fresh parsley sprigs
4 fresh thyme sprigs
6 black peppercorns
1 tsp salt

TO GARNISH
lemon slices
fresh flat-leaved parsley sprigs

1 First, make the court-bouillon. Place all the ingredients in a large saucepan and bring to the boil over a low heat. Cover and simmer for 30 minutes. Strain the liquid through a fine sieve into a clean pan. Bring to the boil and boil rapidly for about 15–20 minutes until reduced to 600 ml/1 pint.

2 Place the trout in a large frying pan. Add the

court-bouillon and bring slowly to the boil. Remove the pan from the heat and set aside to cool.

3 Meanwhile, make the watercress mayonnaise. Put the egg yolk, mustard, watercress and vinegar into a food processor or blender and blend for 30 seconds. Add the oil, drop by drop, until the mixture begins to thicken. The add the oil in a steady stream until it is all incorporated. Add a little hot water if the mixture seems too thick. Season to taste and set aside.

4 Cook the potatoes in plenty of boiling salted

water for 12–15 minutes until soft and tender. Drain well and refresh them under cold running water. Set the potatoes aside until cold.

5 When the potatoes are cold, cut them in half if they are large, and toss with the watercress mayonnaise, finely chopped spring onions and hard-boiled egg.

6 Carefully lift the fish from the poaching liquid and drain on kitchen paper. Carefully pull the skin away from each of the trout. Place them on 4 serving plates with the potato salad, garnish with lemon slices and flat-leaved parsley and serve.

Baked Salmon

Serves 8–10

INGREDIENTS

3 kg/6 lb 8 oz salmon filleted

8 tbsp chopped fresh mixed herbs

2 tbsp green peppercorns in brine, drained

1 tsp finely grated lime rind

6 tbsp dry vermouth or dry white wine

salt and pepper

parsley sprigs, to garnish

RED PEPPER RELISH

125 ml/4 fl oz white wine vinegar

300 ml/10 fl oz light olive oil

1–2 tsp chilli sauce, to taste

6 spring onions, finely sliced

1 orange or red pepper, deseeded and finely diced

1 tbsp chopped fresh flat-leaved parsley

2 tbsp chopped fresh chives

CAPER AND GHERKIN MAYONNAISE

350 ml/12 fl oz good-quality mayonnaise

3 tbsp chopped capers

3 tbsp finely chopped gherkins

2 tbsp chopped fresh flat-leaved parsley

1 tbsp Dijon mustard

1 Wash and dry the salmon fillets and place 1 fillet, skin side down, on a large sheet of oiled foil. Mix together the chopped herbs, peppercorns and lime rind and spread over the top of the fish. Season to taste with salt and pepper and lay the second fillet on top, skin side up. Drizzle over the vermouth or white wine. Wrap the foil over the salmon, twisting well to make a loose-fitting, but tightly sealed parcel.

2 Transfer the foil parcel to a large baking tray and bake in a preheated oven, 120°C/250°F/Gas Mark ½, for 1½ hours until tender (test with the point of a knife). Remove from the oven and set aside to rest for about 20 minutes before serving.

3 Meanwhile, make the red pepper relish. Whisk together the vinegar, olive oil and chilli sauce to taste. Add the spring onions, orange or red pepper, parsley and chives. Season and set aside.

4 To make the caper and gherkin mayonnaise, mix all the ingredients together and set aside.

5 Unwrap the cooked salmon and slice thickly. Arrange the slices on a large serving platter and serve with the red pepper relish and caper and gherkin mayonnaise. Garnish with fresh parsley sprigs.

Barbecued Monkfish

Serves 4

INGREDIENTS

4 tbsp olive oil
grated rind of 1 lime
2 tsp Thai fish sauce
2 garlic cloves, crushed

1 tsp grated fresh root ginger
2 tbsp chopped fresh basil
700 g/1 lb 9 oz monkfish fillet,
    cut into chunks

2 limes, each cut into 6 wedges
salt and pepper
fresh basil sprigs, to garnish

1 Mix together the olive oil, lime rind, Thai fish sauce, garlic, ginger and basil in a large bowl. Season with salt and pepper and set aside.

2 Wash the fish and pat dry with kitchen paper. Add it to the marinade and mix thoroughly to coat. Cover with clingfilm and set aside to marinate for 2 hours, stirring occasionally.

3 If you are using bamboo skewers, soak them in cold water for 30 minutes to prevent them from charring.

Then, lift the monkfish pieces from the marinade and thread them on to the skewers, alternating with the lime wedges.

4 Transfer the skewers, either to a hot barbecue or to a preheated ridged grill pan or to a preheated grill. Cook for 5–6 minutes, turning regularly, until the fish is tender. Serve immediately, garnished with basil sprigs.

VARIATION

You could use any type of white fleshed fish for this recipe but sprinkle the pieces with salt and leave for 2 hours to firm the flesh, before rinsing, drying and then adding to the marinade.

Cod & Chips

Serves 4

INGREDIENTS

900 g/2 lb old potatoes	BATTER	MAYONNAISE
4 x 175 g/6 oz thick cod fillets	15 g/½ oz fresh yeast	1 egg yolk
vegetable oil, for deep-frying	300 ml/10 fl oz beer	1 tsp wholegrain mustard
salt and pepper	225 g/8 oz plain flour	1 tbsp lemon juice
fresh parsley sprigs, to garnish	2 tsp salt	200 ml/7 fl oz light olive oil
lemon wedges, to serve		salt and pepper

1 For the batter, cream the yeast with a little of the beer to a smooth paste. Gradually stir in the rest of the beer. Sift the plain flour and salt into a bowl, make a well in the centre and add the yeast mixture. Gradually whisk to a smooth batter. Cover and leave at room temperature for 1 hour.

2 For the mayonnaise, put the egg yolk, mustard, lemon juice and seasoning into a food processor. Blend for 30 seconds until frothy. Begin adding the olive oil, drop by drop, until the mixture begins to thicken. Continue adding the oil in a slow, steady stream until all the oil has been incorporated. Taste for seasoning. Thin with a little hot water if the mayonnaise is too thick. Refrigerate until needed.

3 For the fish and chips, cut the potatoes into chips about 1.5 cm/1 inch thick. Heat a large saucepan half filled with vegetable oil to 140°C/275°F or until a cube of bread browns in 1 minute. Cook the chips, in 2 batches, for about 5 minutes, until they are cooked through but not browned. Place the chips to drain on kitchen paper and set aside.

4 Increase the temperature of the oil to 160°C/ 325°F or until a cube of bread browns in 45 seconds. Season the fish with salt and pepper then dip into the batter. Fry 2 pieces at a time for 7–8 minutes until deep golden brown and cooked through. Drain thoroughly on kitchen paper and keep warm while you are cooking the remaining fish. Keep these warm while you finish cooking the chips.

5 Increase the temperature of the oil to 190°C/ 375°F or until a cube of bread browns in 30 seconds. Fry the chips again, in 2 batches, for 2–3 minutes until crisp and golden. Drain on kitchen paper and sprinkle with salt.

6 Serve the fish with the chips and mayonnaise. Serve while still piping hot, garnished with fresh parsley sprigs and accompanied by lemon wedges.

Haddock Goujons

Serves 4

INGREDIENTS

175 g/6 oz herb focaccia bread
700 g/1 lb 9 oz skinless
   haddock fillet
2–3 tbsp plain flour
2 eggs, lightly beaten
vegetable oil, for deep-frying

parsley sprigs, to garnish
lemon wedges, to serve

TARTARE SAUCE
1 egg yolk
1 tsp Dijon mustard
2 tsp white wine vinegar

150 ml/5 fl oz light olive oil
1 tsp finely chopped green olives
1 tsp finely chopped gherkins
1 tsp finely chopped capers
2 tsp chopped fresh chives
2 tsp chopped fresh parsley
salt and pepper

1 Put the focaccia into the bowl of a food processor and process to fine crumbs. Set aside. Thinly slice the haddock fillet widthways into fingers. Put the flour, beaten eggs and breadcrumbs into separate bowls. Dip the haddock fingers into the flour, then into the eggs and, finally, into the breadcrumbs to coat. Lay on a plate and refrigerate for 30 minutes.

2 For the tartare sauce, put the egg yolk, mustard, vinegar and seasoning into

the clean bowl of a food processor. Blend for about 30 seconds until frothy. Begin adding the olive oil, drop by drop, until the mixture begins to thicken. Continue adding the olive oil in a slow, steady stream until all the oil is incorporated.

3 Scrape from the food processor bowl into a small mixing bowl and stir in the olives, gherkins, capers, chives and parsley. Check for seasoning. Add a little hot water if the sauce is too thick.

4 Heat a large pan half filled with vegetable oil to 190°C/375°F or until a cube of bread browns in 30 seconds. Cook the goujons, in batches of 3 or 4, for 3–4 minutes until the crumbs are browned and crisp and the fish is cooked. Drain on the kitchen paper and keep warm while you cook the remaining fish.

5 Serve the haddock goujons immediately, with the tartare sauce and lemon wedges.

Swordfish Steaks

Serves 4

INGREDIENTS

4 x swordfish steaks, about
150 g/5½ oz each
4 tbsp olive oil
1 garlic clove, crushed
1 tsp lemon rind
lemon wedges, to garnish

SALSA VERDE
25 /1 oz fresh flat-leaved
parsley leaves
15 g/½ oz mixed herbs, such as
basil, mint and chives
1 garlic clove, chopped
1 tbsp capers, drained and rinsed
1 tbsp green peppercorns in
brine, drained

4 anchovies in oil, drained and
roughly chopped
1 tsp Dijon mustard
125 ml/4 fl oz extra-virgin
olive oil
salt and pepper

1 Wash the swordfish steaks, pat dry with kitchen paper and arrange in a non-metallic dish. Mix together the olive oil, garlic and lemon rind. Pour over the swordfish steaks and leave to marinate for 2 hours.

2 For the salsa verde, put the parsley leaves, mixed herbs, garlic, capers, green peppercorns, anchovies, mustard and olive oil into a food processor or blender. Process to a smooth paste, adding a little warm water if necessary. Season to taste and set aside.

3 Remove the swordfish steaks from the marinade. Cook on a barbecue or preheated ridged grill pan for 2–3 minutes each side until tender. Serve immediately with the salsa verde and lemon wedges.

VARIATION

Any firm fleshed-fish will do this recipe. Try tuna or even shark instead.

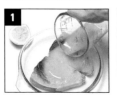

Swordfish or Tuna Fajitas

Serves 4

INGREDIENTS

3 tbsp olive oil
2 tsp chilli powder
1 tsp ground cumin
pinch of cayenne pepper
1 garlic clove, crushed
900 g/2 lb swordfish or tuna
1 red pepper, deseeded and
    thinly sliced
1 yellow pepper, deseeded and
    thinly sliced

2 courgettes, cut into batons
1 large onion, thinly sliced
12 soft flour tortillas
1 tbsp lemon juice
3 tbsp chopped fresh coriander
salt and pepper
150 ml/5 fl oz soured cream,
    to serve

GUACAMOLE
1 large avocado
1 tomato, peeled, deseeded
    and diced
1 garlic clove, crushed
dash of Tabasco sauce
2 tbsp lemon juice
salt and pepper

1 Mix together the oil, chilli powder, cumin, cayenne and garlic. Cut the swordfish or tuna into chunks and mix with the marinade. Set aside for 1–2 hours.

2 Heat a large frying pan until hot. Add the fish and its marinade to the pan and cook for 2 minutes, stirring occasionally, until the

fish begins to brown. Add the red pepper, yellow pepper, courgettes and onion and continue cooking for a further 5 minutes until the vegetables have softened, but are still firm.

3 Meanwhile, warm the flour tortillas in a low oven or in a microwave according to the instructions on the packet.

4 To make the guacamole, mash the avocado until fairly smooth, then stir in the tomato, garlic, Tabasco sauce, lemon juice and seasoning.

5 Add the lemon juice, coriander and seasoning to the fish mixture. Spoon some of the mixture on to each tortilla. Top with guacamole and a spoonful of soured cream and roll up.

Smoked Fish Pie

Serves 6

INGREDIENTS

2 tbsp olive oil

1 onion, finely chopped

1 leek, thinly sliced

1 carrot, diced

1 celery stick, diced

115 g/4 oz button mushrooms,
    halved if large

grated rind 1 lemon

375 g/12 oz skinless smoked cod
    or haddock fillet, cubed

375 g/12 oz skinless white fish
    such as haddock, hake or
    monkfish, cubed

225 g/8 oz cooked peeled prawns

2 tbsp chopped fresh parsley

1 tbsp chopped fresh dill

steamed baby vegetables, to serve

SAUCE

4 tbsp butter

40 g/1½ oz plain flour

1 tsp mustard powder

600 ml/1 pint milk

85 g/3 oz Gruyère cheese,
    freshly grated

TOPPING

750 g/1½ lb potatoes, unpeeled

4 tbsp butter, melted

25 g/1 oz Gruyère cheese, grated

salt and pepper

1 To make the sauce, melt the butter in a large saucepan and stir in the flour and mustard powder. Stir until smooth and cook over a very low heat for 2 minutes without colouring. Slowly beat in the milk until smooth. Simmer gently for 2 minutes, then stir in the cheese until melted and smooth. Remove the pan from the heat and put some cling film over the surface of

the sauce to prevent a skin from forming. Set aside.

2 Meanwhile, for the topping, boil the whole potatoes in plenty of salted water for 15 minutes. Drain well and set aside until cool enough to handle.

3 Heat the olive oil in a clean pan and add the onion. Cook for 5 minutes until softened. Add the leek, carrot, celery and mushrooms and cook a further 10 minutes until the vegetables have softened. Stir in the lemon rind and cook briefly.

4 Add the softened vegetables with the fish,

prawns, parsley and dill to the sauce. Season with salt and pepper and transfer to a greased 1.7 litre/3 pint ovenproof dish.

5 Peel the cooled potatoes and grate coarsely. Mix with the melted butter. Cover the filling with the grated potato and sprinkle with the grated Gruyère cheese.

6 Cover loosely with foil and bake in a preheated oven, 200°C/400°F/Gas Mark 6, for 30 minutes. Remove the foil and bake a further 30 minutes until the topping is tender and golden. Serve immediately with steamed baby vegetables.

Hake Steaks with Chermoula

Serves 4

INGREDIENTS

4 x 225g/8 oz hake steaks
115 g/4 oz stoned green olives
lemon slices, to garnish
steamed green beans, to serve

MARINADE
6 tbsp finely chopped fresh
   coriander
6 tbsp finely chopped fresh
   parsley
6 garlic cloves, crushed

1 tbsp ground cumin
1 tsp ground coriander
1 tbsp paprika
pinch cayenne pepper
150 ml/5 fl oz fresh lemon juice
300 ml/10 fl oz olive oil

1 To make the marinade, mix together the chopped coriander, parsley, garlic, cumin, ground coriander, paprika, cayenne, lemon juice and olive oil in a large bowl.

2 Wash the hake steaks, pat dry with kitchen paper and place in an ovenproof dish. Pour the marinade over the fish and set aside for at least 1 hour and preferably overnight.

3 Before cooking, scatter the olives over the fish. Cover the dish with foil.

4 Cook in a preheated oven, 160°C/325°F/Gas Mark 3, for 35–40 minutes until the fish is tender. Garnish with lemon slices and serve with green beans.

VARIATION

Remove the fish from the marinade and dust with seasoned flour. Fry in oil or clarified butter until golden. Warm through the marinade, but do not boil, and serve as a sauce with lemon slices.

Stuffed Mackerel

Serves 4

INGREDIENTS

4 large mackerel, cleaned
1 tbsp olive oil
1 small onion, thinly sliced
1 tsp ground cinnamon

½ tsp ground ginger
2 tbsp raisins
2 tbsp pine kernels, toasted
8 vine leaves in brine, drained

salt and pepper
selection of salads, such as rice
   salad, tomato salad and
   mixed leaves, to serve

1 Wash the mackerel inside and out, pat dry and set aside. Heat the oil in a small frying pan and add the onion. Cook over a low heat, stirring occasionally, for 5 minutes until softened. Stir in the cinnamon and ginger and cook for 30 seconds before adding the raisins and pine kernels. Remove the pan from the heat and set aside to cool.

2 Stuff each of the fish with a quarter of the stuffing mixture. Wrap each fish in 2 vine leaves, securing with cocktail sticks.

3 Cook on a preheated barbecue or ridged grill pan for 5 minutes on each side until the vine leaves have scorched and the fish is tender. Garnish with lemon slices and serve immediately with salad.

VARIATION

This stuffing works equally well with many other fish, including sea bass and red mullet.

Tuna Fishcakes

Serves 4

INGREDIENTS

225 g/8 oz potatoes, cubed
1 tbsp olive oil
1 large shallot, finely chopped
1 garlic clove, finely chopped
1 tsp thyme leaves
2 x 200 g/7 oz cans tuna in olive oil, drained

grated rind ½ lemon
1 tbsp chopped fresh parsley
2–3 tbsp plain flour
1 egg, lightly beaten
115 g/4 oz fresh breadcrumbs
vegetable oil, for shallow frying
salt and pepper

QUICK TOMATO SAUCE
2 tbsp olive oil
1 garlic clove, crushed
400 g/14 oz can chopped tomatoes
½ tsp sugar
grated rind ½ lemon
1 tbsp chopped fresh basil
salt and pepper

1 For the tuna fishcakes, cook the potatoes in plenty of boiling salted water for 12–15 minutes until tender. Mash, leaving a few lumps, and set aside.

2 Heat the olive oil in a small frying pan and cook the shallot gently for 5 minutes until softened. Add the garlic and thyme leaves and cook for a further minute. Allow to cool slightly, then add to the potatoes with the tuna,

lemon rind and parsley and season to taste with salt and pepper. Mix together well but leave some texture.

3 Form the mixture into 6–8 cakes. Dip the cakes first in the flour, then the egg and, finally, the breadcrumbs to coat. Refrigerate for 30 minutes.

4 Meanwhile, make the tomato sauce. Put the olive oil, garlic, tomatoes, sugar, lemon rind, basil and

seasoning into a saucepan and bring to the boil. Cover and simmer gently for 30 minutes. Uncover and simmer for a further 15 minutes until thickened.

5 Heat enough oil in a frying pan to cover the bottom generously. Add the fishcakes, in batches, and fry for 3–4 minutes on each side until golden and crisp. Drain on kitchen paper while you fry the remaining fishcakes. Serve with the tomato sauce.

Sardines with Pesto

Serves 4

INGREDIENTS

16 large sardines, scaled
   and gutted
50 g/1¾ oz fresh basil leaves
2 garlic cloves, crushed
2 tbsp pine kernels, toasted

50 g/1¾ oz freshly grated
   Parmesan cheese
150 ml/5 fl oz olive oil
salt and pepper
lemon slices, to serve

1 Wash the sardines inside and out, pat dry on kitchen paper and arrange on a grill pan.

2 Put the basil leaves, garlic and pine kernels in a food processor. Blend until finely chopped. Scrape out of the food processor and stir in the Parmesan and oil. Season to taste with salt and pepper.

3 Spread a little of the pesto over one side of the sardines and place under a preheated hot grill for 3 minutes. Turn the fish, spread with more pesto and grill for a further 3 minutes until the sardines are cooked and piping hot.

4 Serve immediately with extra pesto and lemon slices.

VARIATION

This treatment will also work well with other small oily fish, such as herrings and pilchards.

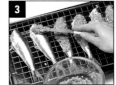

Salmon Frittata

Serves 6

INGREDIENTS

250 g/9 oz skinless salmon fillet
3 fresh thyme sprigs
fresh parsley sprig plus 2 tbsp
    chopped fresh parsley
5 black peppercorns
½ small onion, sliced
½ celery stick, sliced
½ carrot, chopped

FRITTATA
175 g/6 oz asparagus spears,
    chopped
85 g/3 oz baby carrots, halved
4 tbsp butter
1 large onion, thinly sliced
1 garlic clove, finely chopped
115 g/4 oz peas, fresh or frozen
8 eggs, lightly beaten

1 tbsp chopped fresh dill
salt and pepper
lemon wedges, to garnish

TO SERVE
crème fraîche
salad
crusty bread

1 Place the salmon in a large saucepan with 1 sprig of the thyme, the parsley sprig, peppercorns, onion, celery and carrot. Cover the vegetables and fish with cold water and bring to the boil over a low heat. Remove the saucepan from the heat and leave to stand for 5 minutes. Lift the fish out of the the poaching liquid, flake the flesh and set aside. Discard the poaching liquid.

2 Bring a large saucepan of salted water to the boil and blanch the asparagus for 2 minutes. Drain and refresh under cold water. Blanch the carrots for 4 minutes. Drain and refresh under cold water. Drain again and pat dry. Set aside.

3 Heat half the butter in a large frying pan and add the onion. Cook over a low heat, stirring occasionally, for 8–10 minutes until softened, but not coloured. Add the

garlic and remaining sprigs of thyme and cook for a further minute. Add the asparagus, carrots and peas and heat through. Remove the pan from the heat.

4 Add the vegetables to the eggs with the chopped parsley, dill, salmon and seasoning and stir briefly. Heat the remaining butter in the pan and return the mixture to the pan. Cover and cook over a low heat for 10 minutes.

5 Cook under a preheated medium grill for a further 5 minutes until set and golden. Serve hot or cold in wedges topped with a spoon of crème fraîche, with salad and crusty bread. Garnish with lemon wedges.

Mixed Seafood Brochettes

Serves 4

INGREDIENTS

225 g/8 oz skinless turbot fillet
225 g/8 oz skinless salmon fillet
8 scallops
8 large tiger prawns
   or langoustines
16 fresh bay leaves
1 lemon, sliced

4 tbsp olive oil
grated rind 1 lemon
4 tbsp chopped mixed herbs such
   as thyme, parsley, chives
   and basil
black pepper

LEMON BUTTER RICE
175 g/6 oz long grain rice
grated rind and juice 1 lemon
4 tbsp butter
salt and pepper

TO GARNISH
lemon wedges
dill sprigs

1 Chop the turbot and salmon fillets into 8 pieces each. Carefully thread the pieces of fish on to 8 skewers, together with the scallops and tiger prawns or langoustines, alternating with the bay leaves and lemon slices. Put the skewers into a non-metallic dish in a single layer if possible.

2 Mix together the olive oil, lemon rind, mixed herbs and black pepper. Pour this mixture over the fish, turning to coat. Cover with clingfilm and set aside to marinate for 2 hours, turning once or twice.

3 For the lemon butter rice, bring a large pan of lightly salted water to the boil and add the rice and lemon rind. Bring back to the boil and simmer over a medium heat for 10–15 minutes until the rice is tender. Drain well and immediately stir in the lemon juice and butter. Season with salt and pepper to taste.

4 Meanwhile, lift the fish brochettes from their marinade and cook on a lighted barbecue or under a preheated hot grill for 8–10 minutes, turning frequently, until cooked through. Serve immediately with the lemon butter rice. Garnish with lemon wedges and dill sprigs.

Char-grilled Scallops

Serves 4

INGREDIENTS

16 king scallops
3 tbsp olive oil
grated rind 1 lime
2 tbsp chopped fresh basil
2 tbsp chopped fresh chives
1 garlic clove, finely chopped
black pepper

JEWELLED COUSCOUS
225 g/ 8 oz couscous
½ red pepper, deseeded
    and halved
½ yellow pepper, deseeded
    and halved
4 tbsp extra-virgin olive oil
115 g/4 oz cucumber, chopped
    into 1 cm/½ inch pieces

3 spring onions, finely chopped
1 tbsp lime juice
2 tbsp shredded fresh basil
salt and pepper

TO GARNISH
basil leaves
lime wedges

1 Clean and trim the scallops as necessary. Place them in a non-metallic dish. Mix together the olive oil, lime rind, basil, chives, garlic and black pepper. Pour the mixture over the scallops, turning to coat, and cover with clingfilm. Set aside to marinate for 2 hours.

2 Cook the couscous according to the packet instructions, omitting any butter recommended. Brush the red and yellow pepper

halves with a little of the olive oil and place under a preheated hot grill for 5–6 minutes, turning once, until the skins are blackened and the flesh is tender. Put into a plastic bag and leave until cool enough to handle. When cool, peel off the skins and chop the flesh into 1 cm/1 inch pieces. Add to the couscous with the remaining olive oil, the cucumber, spring onions and lime juice and season to taste with salt and pepper. Set aside.

3 Lift the scallops from the marinade and thread on to 4 skewers. Cook on a lighted barbecue or preheated ridged grill pan for 1 minute on each side, until charred and firm but not quite cooked through. Remove from the heat and allow to rest for 2 minutes.

4 Stir the shredded basil into the couscous, divide on to plates, and put a skewer on each. Garnish with basil leaves and lime wedges.

Prawn Rostis

Serves 4

INGREDIENTS

350 g/12 oz potatoes
350 g/12 oz celeriac
1 carrot
½ small onion
225 g/8 oz cooked peeled
   prawns, defrosted if frozen
   and well drained on
   kitchen paper
4 tbsp plain flour

1 egg, lightly beaten
vegetable oil, for frying
salt and pepper

CHERRY TOMATO SALSA
225 g/8 oz mixed cherry
   tomatoes such as baby plum,
   yellow, orange and
   pear, quartered

½ small mango, finely diced
1 red chilli, deseeded and
   finely chopped
½ small red onion, finely chopped
1 tbsp chopped fresh coriander
1 tbsp chopped fresh chives
2 tbsp olive oil
2 tsp lemon juice
salt and pepper

1 For the salsa, mix together the tomatoes, mango, chilli, red onion, coriander, chives, olive oil and lemon juice and season to taste. Set aside for the flavours to infuse.

2 Using a food processor or the fine blade of a box grater, finely grate the potatoes, celeriac, carrot and onion. Mix together with the prawns, flour and egg.

Season well with salt and pepper and set aside.

3 Divide the prawn mixture into 8 equal pieces. Press each into a greased 10 cm/4 inch metal cutter (if you have only 1 cutter, simply shape the rostis individually).

4 In a large frying pan, heat a shallow layer of vegetable oil. Transfer the

prawn cakes, still in the cutters, to the frying pan , in batches if necessary. When the oil sizzles underneath, remove the cutter. Fry over a low heat, pressing down with a spatula, for 6–8 minutes on each side, until crisp and browned and the vegetables are tender. Drain well on kitchen paper. Serve the prawn rostis immediately while they are still hot with the tomato salsa.

Moules Marinières

Serves 4

INGREDIENTS

900 g/2 lb live mussels
2 shallots, finely chopped
2 garlic cloves, finely chopped
150 ml/5 fl oz white wine
2 tbsp chopped fresh parsley
salt and pepper

CHIPS
900 g/2 lb potatoes
vegetable oil, for deep-frying
salt

TO SERVE (OPTIONAL)
lemon wedges
mayonnaise

1 Clean the mussels by scrubbing or scraping the shells and pulling off any beards. Discard any mussels with broken shells or that do not close when tapped sharply on a work surface.

2 For the chips, cut the potatoes into thin strips, about 1 cm/1 inch thick. Fill a large saucepan or deep-fat fryer about one-third full of vegetable oil and heat to 140°C/ 275°F or until a cube of bread browns in 1 minute. Add the chips, in 3 batches, and cook for 5–6 minutes until the chips are tender but not browned. Drain well on kitchen paper.

3 Put the mussels in a large saucepan with the shallots, garlic and white wine. Cover and cook over a high heat, shaking the pan vigorously from time to time, for 3–4 minutes until all the mussels have opened. Discard any mussels that remain closed. Add the parsley and taste for seasoning. Set aside and keep warm while you finish the cooking the chips.

4 Increase the temperature of the oil to 190°C/375°F, or until a cube of bread browns in 30 seconds. Cook the chips, again in 3 batches, for 2–3 minutes until golden and crisp. Drain well on kitchen paper and sprinkle with salt.

5 Divide the mussels between 4 large serving bowls. Divide the chips between smaller bowls or plates and serve with lemon wedges and plenty of mayonnaise for dipping the chips, if liked.

Provençal Mussels

Serves 4

INGREDIENTS

900 g/2 lb live mussels
3 tbsp olive oil
1 onion, finely chopped
3 garlic cloves, finely chopped
2 tsp fresh thyme leaves
150 ml/ 5 fl oz red wine

2 x 400 g/14 oz cans
    chopped tomatoes
2 tbsp chopped fresh parsley
salt and pepper
crusty bread, to serve

1 Clean the mussels by scrubbing or scraping the shells and pulling off any beards. Discard any mussels with broken shells or that do not close when tapped sharply on a work surface. Put the mussels in a large saucepan with just the water that clings to their shells. Cover and cook over a high heat for 3–4 minutes until all the mussels have opened. Discard any mussels that remain closed. Drain well, reserving the cooking liquid. Set aside.

2 Heat the oil in a large saucepan and add the onion. Cook over a low heat, stirring occasionally, for about 8–10 minutes until softened, but not coloured. Add the garlic and thyme and cook for a further 1 minute. Add the red wine and simmer rapidly until reduced and syrupy. Add the tomatoes and strained, reserved mussel cooking liquid and bring to the boil. Cover and simmer for 30 minutes. Uncover and cook for a further 15 minutes.

3 Add the mussels and cook for a further 5 minutes until heated through. Stir in the parsley, season to taste with salt and pepper and serve with plenty of fresh crusty bread.

VARIATION

Replace the mussels with an equal quantity of clams.

Pasta, Rice & other Grains

Nutritionists today recommend a diet high in complex carbohydrates, which include pasta, rice, potatoes, breads and grains. A diet based around this food group ensures high energy levels without any dips in blood sugar levels, which can lead to bingeing.

This chapter includes a variety of dishes based on these foods. The most popular of these has to be pasta and there are a number of pasta dishes here. There are also a variety of skill levels catered for, from very simple pasta dishes, such as Spaghettini with Crab and Linguini with Sardines, to more complicated dishes, such as homemade Squid Ink Pasta, Fideua and Seafood Lasagne.

There are also pies and pasties, such as Herring & Potato Pie and Fish Pasties, as well as rice dishes, including Jambalaya, Lobster Risotto and Prawn & Asparagus Risotto.

Dishes using other grains include Buckwheat Pancakes with Smoked Salmon & Crème Fraîche, Fish & Bread Soup and Pizza Marinara.

Tagliatelle with Broccoli & Anchovies

Serves 4

INGREDIENTS

6 tbsp olive oil
50 g/1¾ oz fresh
   white breadcrumbs
450g/1 lb broccoli, cut into
   small florets

350 g/12 oz dried tagliatelle
4 canned anchovy fillets, drained
   and chopped
2 garlic cloves, sliced
grated rind of 1 lemon

large pinch of chilli flakes
salt and pepper
freshly grated Parmesan cheese,
   to serve

1 Heat 2 tablespoons of the olive oil in a frying pan over a medium heat and add the breadcrumbs. Stir-fry for 4–5 minutes until golden and crisp. Drain on kitchen paper.

2 Bring a large pan of salted water to the boil and add the broccoli. Blanch for 3 minutes, then drain, reserving the water. Refresh the broccoli under cold water and drain again. Gently pat dry on kitchen paper. Set aside.

3 Bring the water back to the boil and add the tagliatelle. Bring back to the boil and cook for 8–10 minutes until tender, but still firm to the bite.

4 Meanwhile, heat another 2 tablespoons of the oil in a large frying pan or wok and add the anchovies. Cook for 1 minute, then mash with a wooden spoon to a paste. Stir in the garlic, lemon rind and chilli flakes and cook over a low heat, stirring occasionally, for 2 minutes.

Add the broccoli and cook for a further 3–4 minutes until hot.

5 Drain the cooked pasta and return to the pan. Add the broccoli mixture with the remaining 2 tbsp of the olive oil and season to taste. Toss together well.

6 Divide the tagliatelle between 4 warmed serving plates. Top with the fried breadcrumbs, sprinkle with grated Parmesan cheese and serve immediately.

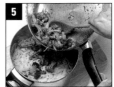

Pasta Puttanesca

Serves 4

INGREDIENTS

3 tbsp extra-virgin olive oil
1 large red onion, finely chopped
4 anchovy fillets, drained
pinch of chilli flakes
2 garlic cloves, finely chopped
400 g/14 oz can

chopped tomatoes
2 tbsp tomato purée
225 g/8 oz dried spaghetti
25 g/1 oz stoned black olives,
    roughly chopped

25 g/1 oz stoned green olives,
    roughly chopped
1 tbsp capers, drained and rinsed
4 sun-dried tomatoes in oil,
    drained and roughly chopped
salt and pepper

1 Heat the olive oil in a saucepan and add the onion, anchovies and chilli flakes. Cook over a low heat, stirring frequently, for 10 minutes until softened and starting to brown. Add the garlic and cook for a further 30 seconds.

2 Add the tomatoes and tomato purée, increase the heat to medium and

bring to the boil. Lower the heat and simmer gently for 10 minutes.

3 Meanwhile, bring a large pan of salted water to the boil. Add the spaghetti, bring back to the boil and cook for 8–10 minutes until tender, but still firm to the bite.

4 Add the olives, capers and sun-dried tomatoes

to the sauce. Simmer for a further 2–3 minutes. Season to taste with salt and pepper.

5 Drain the pasta well, return to the pan and stir in the sauce. Toss thoroughly to mix. Serve immediately.

Seafood Lasagne

Serves 4

INGREDIENTS

4 tbsp butter, plus extra
    for greasing
5 tbsp flour
1 tsp mustard powder
600 ml/1 pint milk
2 tbsp olive oil
1 onion, chopped

2 garlic cloves, finely chopped
1 tbsp fresh thyme leaves
450 g/1 lb mixed
    mushrooms, sliced
150 ml/5 fl oz white wine
400 g/14 oz can
    chopped tomatoes

450 g/1 lb mixed skinless white
    fish fillets, cubed
225 g/8 oz fresh scallops, trimmed
4–6 sheets fresh lasagne
225 g/8 oz mozzarella
    cheese, diced
salt and pepper

1 Melt the butter in a saucepan. Add the flour and mustard powder and stir until smooth. Cook over a low heat for 2 minutes without colouring. Gradually add the milk, whisking until smooth. Bring to the boil and simmer for 2 minutes. Remove from the heat and set aside. Cover the surface of the sauce with clingfilm to prevent a skin from forming.

2 Heat the oil in a frying pan and add the onion, garlic and thyme. Cook over a low heat, stirring occasionally, for 5 minutes until softened. Add the mushrooms and fry for a further 5 minutes. Stir in the wine and boil rapidly until almost evaporated. Stir in the tomatoes. Bring to the boil and simmer, covered, for 15 minutes. Season to taste with salt and pepper and set aside.

3 Lightly grease a lasagne dish. Spoon half the tomato sauce over the base of the dish and top with half the fish and scallops.

4 Layer half the lasagne over the fish, pour over half the white sauce and add half the diced mozzarella. Repeat these layers, finishing with the white sauce and mozzarella.

5 Bake in a preheated oven, 200°C/400°F/Gas Mark 6, for 35–40 minutes until the top is bubbling and golden and the fish is cooked through. Remove from the oven and leave to stand for 10 minutes before serving straight from the dish.

Spaghetti al Vongole

Serves 4

INGREDIENTS

900 g/2 lb live clams, scrubbed
2 tbsp olive oil
1 large onion, finely chopped
2 garlic cloves, finely chopped

1 tsp fresh thyme leaves
150 ml/5 fl oz white wine
400 g/14 oz can
    chopped tomatoes

350 g/12 oz dried spaghetti
1 tbsp chopped fresh parsley
salt and pepper

1 Put the clams into a large saucepan with just the water clinging to their shells. Cook, covered, over a high heat for 3–4 minutes, shaking the pan occasionally, until all the clams have opened. Remove from the heat and strain, reserving the cooking liquid. Discard any clams that remain closed. Set aside.

2 Heat the oil in a saucepan and add the onion. Cook for 10 minutes over a low heat until softened, but not coloured. Add the garlic and thyme and cook for a further 30 seconds. Increase the heat and add the white wine. Simmer rapidly until reduced and syrupy. Add the tomatoes and reserved clam cooking liquid. Cover and simmer for 15 minutes. Uncover and simmer for a further 15 minutes until thickened. Season to taste.

3 Meanwhile, bring a large saucepan of lightly salted water to the boil. Add the pasta, bring back to the boil and cook for 8–10 minutes until tender, but still firm to the bite.

4 Add the clams to the tomato sauce and heat through for 2–3 minutes. Add the parsley and stir well. Add the tomato sauce to the pasta and toss together until the spaghetti is well coated in sauce. Serve immediately.

COOK'S TIP

If you are able to get only very large clams, reserve a few in their shells to garnish and shell the rest.

Linguini with Sardines

SERVES 4

INGREDIENTS

8 sardines, filleted	1 tsp chilli flakes	2 tbsp pine kernels, toasted
1 fennel bulb	350 g/12 oz dried linguine	2 tbsp chopped fresh parsley
4 tbsp olive oil	½ tsp finely grated lemon rind	salt and pepper
3 garlic cloves, sliced	1 tbsp lemon juice	

1 Wash and dry the sardine fillets. Roughly chop into large pieces and set aside. Trim the fennel bulb and slice very thinly.

2 Heat 2 tablespoons of the olive oil in a large frying pan and add the garlic and chilli flakes. Cook for 1 minute, then add the fennel. Cook over a medium high heat, stirring frequently, for 4–5 minutes until softened. Add the sardine pieces and cook for a further 3–4 minutes until just cooked and tender.

3 Meanwhile, bring a large saucepan of lightly salted water to the boil. Add the pasta, bring back to the boil and cook for 8–10 minutes until tender but still firm to the bite. Drain well and return to the pan.

4 Add the lemon rind, lemon juice, pine kernels and parsley to the sardines, season to taste with salt and pepper and toss together. Add to the pasta with the remaining olive oil and toss together gently. Serve while the pasta is still hot.

COOK'S TIP

Reserve a couple of tablespoons of the pasta cooking water and add to the pasta with the sauce if the mixture seems a little dry.

Crab Ravioli

Serves 4

INGREDIENTS

225 g/8 oz strong white bread
  flour, or type '00' Italian
  pasta flour
1 tsp salt
2 eggs, plus 1 egg yolk
1 tbsp olive oil
225 g/8 oz raw prawns,
  finely chopped
225 g/8 oz white crab meat
1 tbsp chopped fresh chervil

1 tbsp chopped fresh chives
1 tbsp chopped fresh parsley
1 tsp grated rind lime
4 tbsp double cream
salt and pepper

RED PEPPER SAUCE
½ large red pepper, deseeded
  and halved
1 tsp olive oil, for brushing

2 tbsp unsalted butter, softened
1 tbsp lime juice
salt and pepper

TO GARNISH
lime wedges
fresh chives

1 To make the pepper sauce, brush the pepper pieces with the olive oil. Place under a preheated hot grill for 3–4 minutes on each side until charred and tender. Remove from the heat and place in a plastic bag until cool enough to handle. Rub off the skin and put the flesh in a food processor or blender. Add the butter and lime juice, season to taste and and process until smooth. Set aside.

2 To make the pasta, sift the flour and salt into a bowl. Make a well in the centre and add the eggs, egg yolk, oil and enough water to make a firm dough. Knead for 5 minutes. Wrap in clingfilm and chill.

3 Meanwhile, mix together the prawns, crab, chervil, chives, parsley, lime rind, cream and seasoning.

4 Divide the pasta dough into 8 pieces. Using a pasta machine, roll out each piece as thinly as possible. Dust the surface liberally with flour and top with 1 sheet of pasta. Place a teaspoon of filling at 2.5 cm/1 inch intervals along the dough. Brush lightly around the

filling with water then place a second sheet of pasta on top.

5 Press down firmly around each mound of filling to seal, then, using a pastry cutter or pasta wheel, cut out the ravioli. Repeat with the remaining pasta and filling, placing the cut-out ravioli on a well-floured tea towel.

6 Bring a large saucepan of lightly salted water to the boil and add the ravioli. Bring back to the boil and cook for 3–4 minutes until the pasta is tender, but still firm to the bite. Drain well and toss immediately with the red pepper sauce. Serve hot, garnished with lime wedges and snipped chives.

Spaghettini with Crab

Serves 4

INGREDIENTS

1 dressed crab, about 450 g/1 lb
   including the shell
350 g/12 oz dried spaghettini
6 tbsp extra-virgin olive oil

1 hot red chilli, deseeded and
   finely chopped
2 garlic cloves, finely chopped
3 tbsp chopped fresh parsley

1 tsp finely grated lemon rind
2 tbsp lemon juice
salt and pepper
lemon wedges, to garnish

1 Scoop the meat from the crab shell into a bowl. Mix the white and brown meat lightly together and set aside.

2 Bring a large saucepan of lightly salted water to the boil. Add the pasta, bring back to the boil and cook for 8–10 minutes until tender, but still firm to the bite. Drain thoroughly and return to the pan.

3 Meanwhile, heat 2 tablespoons of the olive oil in a frying pan. Add the chilli and garlic and cook for 30 seconds before adding the crab meat, parsley, lemon rind and lemon juice. Stir-fry for a further minute until the crab is just heated through.

4 Add the crab mixture to the pasta with the remaining olive oil and season to taste with salt and pepper. Toss together thoroughly and serve immediately, garnished with lemon wedges.

COOK'S TIP

If you prefer to buy your own fresh crab you will need a large crab weighing about 1 kg/2 lb 4 oz.

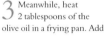

Squid Ink Pasta

Serves 4

INGREDIENTS

450 g/1 lb squid with their ink
300 g/10½ oz strong white bread
    flour or Italian type '00'
    pasta flour
100 g/3½ oz fine semolina

2 eggs
SAUCE
4 tbsp olive oil
2 garlic cloves, finely chopped
1 tsp paprika

3 plum tomatoes, peeled,
    deseeded and diced
150 ml/5 fl oz white wine
1 tbsp chopped fresh parsley
salt and pepper

1 To prepare the squid and its ink, carefully grasp the head and tentacles of the squid and pull to remove all the innards. The ink sac lies at the furthest point from the tentacles and is a silverish tube – be careful to keep it intact. Cut the ink sac away from the innards and set aside. Cut the tentacles just below the beak and discard the remaining innards. Remove the quill from the body and remove the wings and skin. Wash the body and tentacles well.

2 Slice the body width-ways into rings and set

aside with the tentacles. Slit open the ink sac and dilute with water to make 50 ml/2 fl oz. Set aside.

3 To make the pasta, sift together the flour and semolina. Make a well in the centre and add the eggs. Using a wooden spoon, draw the flour and eggs together. Gradually add the squid ink – you may not need it all. Mix to a firm dough. Add a little more water if it seems too stiff and a little more flour if it seems too wet. Alternatively, put all the ingredients in the bowl of a mixer fitted with a kneading hook and mix together. Knead the dough for 10 minutes until smooth and elastic. The dough should have the feel of soft leather and be neither sticky nor should it break easily. Wrap in clingfilm and set aside for 30 minutes.

4 Using a pasta machine, thinly roll out the dough and cut into thin ribbons. Hang to dry.

5 Meanwhile, make the sauce. Heat the oil in a saucepan and add the garlic and paprika. Fry over a medium heat for 30 seconds. Add the squid and cook for 4–5 minutes until lightly browned and firm. Add the tomatoes and cook for 3–4 minutes until collapsed. Lower the heat, add the white wine and simmer for 15 minutes. Stir in the parsley and season to taste.

6 Meanwhile, bring a large pan of salted water to the boil and add the pasta. Cook for 2–3 minutes until tender, but still firm to the bite, then drain thoroughly. Turn into a large serving bowl, toss with the sauce and serve.

Fideua

Serves 4

INGREDIENTS

3 tbsp olive oil
1 large onion, chopped
2 garlic cloves, finely chopped
pinch of saffron, crushed
½ tsp paprika
3 tomatoes, peeled, deseeded and chopped

350 g/12 oz egg vermicelli, broken roughly into 5 cm/2 inch lengths
150 ml/5 fl oz white wine
300 ml/10 fl oz fish stock
12 large raw prawns
18 live mussels, scrubbed and bearded

350 g/12 oz cleaned squid, cut into rings
18 large clams, scrubbed
2 tbsp chopped fresh parsley
salt and pepper
lemon wedges, to serve

1 Heat the oil in a large, heavy-based frying pan or paella pan. Add the onion and cook over a low heat, stirring occasionally, for 5 minutes until softened. Add the garlic and cook for a further 30 seconds. Add the saffron and paprika and stir well. Add the tomatoes and cook for 2–3 minutes until they have collapsed.

2 Add the vermicelli and stir well. Increase the heat, add the wine and boil rapidly until absorbed.

3 Add the fish stock, prawns, mussels, squid and clams. Stir and return to a low simmer for 10 minutes until the prawns and squid are cooked through and the mussels and clams have opened. The stock should be almost completely absorbed.

4 Stir in the parsley and season to taste with salt and pepper. Spoon into warm bowls, garnish with lemon wedges and serve.

VARIATION

Use whatever combination of seafood you prefer. Try langoustines, prawns and monkfish.

Thai Noodles

Serves 4

INGREDIENTS

350 g/12 oz cooked, peeled
   tiger prawns
115 g/4 oz flat rice noodles or
   rice vermicelli
4 tbsp vegetable oil
2 garlic cloves, finely chopped

1 egg
2 tbsp lemon juice
4½ tsp Thai fish sauce
½ tsp sugar
2 tbsp chopped, roasted peanuts
½ tsp cayenne pepper

2 spring onions, cut into 2.5 cm/
   1 inch pieces
50 g/1¾ oz fresh beansprouts
1 tbsp chopped fresh coriander
lemon wedges, to garnish

1 Drain the prawns on kitchen paper to remove excess moisture. Set aside. Cook the rice noodles or rice vermicelli according to the packet instructions. Drain well and set aside.

2 Heat the oil in a wok or large frying pan and add the garlic. Stir-fry until just golden. Add the egg and stir quickly to break it up. Cook for a few seconds.

3 Add the prawns and noodles, scraping down the sides of the pan to ensure

they are thoroughly mixed with the egg and garlic.

4 Add the lemon juice, Thai fish sauce, sugar, half the peanuts, the cayenne pepper, spring onions and half the beansprouts, stirring quickly all the time. Cook over a high heat, stirring constantly for a further 2 minutes until everything is heated through.

5 Turn on to a warm serving plate. Top with the remaining peanuts and beansprouts and sprinkle

with the coriander. Serve immediately, garnished with lemon wedges.

VARIATION

This is a basic dish to which lots of different cooked seafood could be added. Cooked squid rings, mussels and langoustines would all work just as well.

Kedgeree

Serves 4

INGREDIENTS

450 g/1 lb undyed smoked
   haddock fillet
2 tbsp olive oil
1 large onion, chopped
2 garlic cloves, finely chopped
½ tsp ground turmeric

½ tsp ground cumin
1 tsp ground coriander
175 g/6 oz basmati rice
4 medium eggs
2 tbsp butter
1 tbsp chopped fresh parsley

TO SERVE
lemon wedges
mango chutney

1 Place the haddock fillet in a large dish, pour boiling water over it and leave for 10 minutes. Lift the fish from the cooking water, discard the skin and bones and flake the flesh. Set aside. Reserve the cooking water.

2 Heat the oil in a large saucepan and add the onion. Cook over a medium heat, stirring occasionally, for 10 minutes until starting to brown. Add the garlic and cook for a further 30 seconds. Add the turmeric, cumin and ground coriander and stir-fry for 30 seconds until the spices smell fragrant. Add the rice and stir well.

3 Measure 350 ml/12 fl oz of the haddock cooking water and add to the pan. Stir well and bring to the boil. Cover and cook over a very low heat for 12–15 minutes until the rice is tender and the stock is absorbed.

4 Meanwhile, bring a small saucepan of water to the boil and add the eggs. Bring back to the boil and cook the eggs for 8 minutes.

Immediately drain the eggs and refresh under cold water to stop any further cooking. Set aside.

5 Add the reserved fish pieces, the butter and parsley to the rice. Turn on to a large serving dish. Shell and quarter the eggs and arrange on top of the rice. Serve immediately with lemon wedges and mango chutney.

A Modern Kedgeree

Serves 4

INGREDIENTS

2 tbsp butter
1 tbsp olive oil
1 onion, finely chopped
1 garlic clove, finely chopped
175 g g/6 oz long-grain rice

400 ml/14 fl oz fish stock
175 g/6 oz skinless, salmon
   fillet, chopped
85 g/3 oz smoked
   salmon, chopped
2 tbsp double cream
2 tbsp chopped fresh dill

3 spring onions, finely chopped
salt and pepper

TO GARNISH
lemon slices
fresh dill sprigs

1 Melt the butter with the oil in a large saucepan. Add the onion and cook over a low heat, stirring occasionally, for 10 minutes until softened, but not coloured. Add the garlic to the pan and cook for a further 30 seconds.

2 Add the rice and cook, stirring constantly, for 2–3 minutes until the grains are coated and transparent. Add the fish stock and stir well to mix. Bring to the boil, cover and simmer very gently for 10 minutes.

3 Add the salmon fillet and the smoked salmon and stir well, adding a little more stock or water if the mixture seems dry. Cook for a further 6–8 minutes until the fish and rice are tender and all the stock is absorbed.

4 Remove the pan from the heat – or make sure that your gas ring is turned off – and stir in the cream, dill and spring onions. Season to taste with salt and pepper, garnish with sprigs of dill and slices of lemon and serve immediately.

COOK'S TIP

Use smoked salmon trimmings for a budget dish.

Jambalaya

Serves 4

INGREDIENTS

2 tbsp vegetable oil
2 onions, roughly chopped
1 green pepper, deseeded and roughly chopped
2 celery sticks, roughly chopped
3 garlic cloves, finely chopped
2 tsp paprika

300 g/10½ oz skinless, boneless chicken breasts, diced
100 g/3½ oz kabanos sausages, diced
3 tomatoes, peeled and chopped
450 g/1 lb long grain rice
850 ml/1½ pints hot chicken or fish stock

1 tsp dried oregano
2 fresh bay leaves
12 large prawn tails
4 spring onions, finely chopped
2 tbsp chopped fresh parsley
salt and pepper

1 Heat the vegetable oil in a large frying pan and add the onions, pepper, celery and garlic. Cook over a low heat, stirring frequently, for 8–10 minutes until all the vegetables have softened. Stir in the paprika and cook for 30 seconds. Add the chicken and kabanos sausages and cook for 8–10 minutes until lightly browned. Add the tomatoes and cook for a further 2–3 minutes until collapsed.

2 Add the rice to the pan and stir well to coat the grains. Pour in the hot stock, add the oregano and bay leaves and stir well. Cover the pan and simmer gently for 10 minutes over a very low heat.

3 Add the prawns and stir gently. Cover the pan again and simmer gently for a further 6–8 minutes until the rice is tender, the prawns are cooked through and most of the liquid is absorbed.

4 Stir in the spring onions, and parsley and season to taste. Serve immediately.

COOK'S TIP

Jambalaya is a dish which has some basic ingredients – onions, green peppers, celery, rice and seasonings – to which you can add whatever meat and fish you have to hand.

Lobster Risotto

Serves 4

INGREDIENTS

1 cooked lobster, about
    400–450 g/14 oz–1 lb
4 tbsp butter
1 tbsp olive oil
1 onion, finely chopped
1 garlic clove, finely chopped

1 tsp fresh thyme leaves
175 g/6 oz arborio rice
600 ml/1 pint hot fish stock
150 ml/5 fl oz sparkling
    white wine

1 tsp green or pink peppercorns
    in brine, drained and roughly
    chopped
1 tbsp chopped fresh parsley

1 To prepare the lobster, remove the claws by twisting. Crack the claws using the back of a large knife and set aside. Split the body lengthways. Remove and discard the intestinal vein which runs down the tail, the stomach sac and the spongy looking gills. Remove the meat from the tail and roughly chop. Set aside with the claws.

2 Heat half the butter and the oil in a large frying pan. Add the onion and cook over a low heat, stirring occasionally, for 4–5 minutes until softened. Add the garlic and cook for 30 seconds. Add the thyme and the rice. Stir well for 1–2 minutes, until the rice grains are well coated in the butter and oil and begins to look translucent.

3 Keep the stock on a low heat. Increase the heat under the frying pan to medium and begin adding the stock, a ladleful at a time, stirring well between additions. Continue until all the stock has been absorbed. This should take 20–25 minutes.

4 Add the lobster meat and claws. Stir in the sparkling wine, increasing the heat. When the wine is absorbed, remove the pan from the heat and stir in the green or pink peppercorns, remaining butter and parsley. Leave to stand for 1 minute then serve immediately.

VARIATION

For a slightly cheaper version substitute 450 g/1 lb prawns for the lobster.

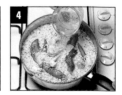

Prawn &
Asparagus Risotto

Serves 4

INGREDIENTS

1.2 litres/2 pints vegetable stock
375 g/12 oz asparagus, cut into
    5 cm/2 inch lengths
2 tbsp olive oil
1 onion, finely chopped

1 garlic clove, finely chopped
375 g/12 oz arborio rice
450 g/1 lb raw tiger prawns,
    peeled and de-veined
2 tbsp olive paste or tapenade

2 tbsp chopped fresh basil
salt and pepper
shavings of Parmesan cheese,
    to garnish

1 Bring the vegetable stock to the boil in a large saucepan. Add the asparagus and cook for 3 minutes until just tender. Strain, reserving the stock, and refresh the asparagus under cold running water. Drain and set aside.

2 Heat the oil in a large frying pan. Add the onion and cook over a low heat, stirring occasionally, for 5 minutes until softened. Add the garlic and cook for a further 30 seconds. Add the rice and stir well for 1–2 minutes until coated with the oil and translucent.

3 Keep the stock on a low heat. Increase the heat under the frying pan to medium and begin adding the stock, a ladleful at a time, stirring well between additions. Continue until almost all the stock has been absorbed. This should take 20–25 minutes.

4 Add the prawns and asparagus with the last ladleful of stock and cook fora further 5 minutes until the prawns and rice are tender and the stock has been absorbed. Remove from the heat.

5 Stir in the olive paste and basil, season to taste with salt and pepper and leave to stand for 1 minute. Serve immediately, garnished with Parmesan shavings.

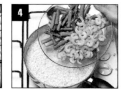

Spicy Coconut Rice
with Monkfish & Peas

Serves 4

INGREDIENTS

1 hot red chilli, deseeded and chopped	4 tbsp olive oil	400g/14 oz can chopped tomatoes
1 tsp crushed chilli flakes	2 tbsp lemon juice	200 ml/7 fl oz coconut milk
2 garlic cloves, chopped	375 g/12 oz monkfish fillet, cut into bite-size pieces	115 g/4 oz peas
2 pinches saffron	1 onion, finely chopped	salt and pepper
3 tbsp roughly chopped mint leaves	225 g/8 oz long grain rice	2 tbsp chopped fresh coriander, to garnish

1 In a food processor or blender, blend together the fresh red chilli, chilli flakes, garlic, saffron, mint leaves, olive oil and lemon juice until finely chopped but not smooth.

2 Put the monkfish into a non-metallic dish and pour over the spice paste, mixing together well. Cover with clingfilm and set aside for 20 minutes to marinate.

3 Heat a large, heavy-based saucepan until very hot. Using a perforated spoon, lift the monkfish from the marinade and add it, in batches, to the hot pan. Cook for 3–4 minutes until browned and firm. Remove with a perforated spoon and set aside.

4 Add the onion and remaining marinade to the same pan and cook over a low heat for 5 minutes until softened and lightly browned. Add the rice and stir until well coated. Add the tomatoes and coconut milk. Bring to the boil, cover and simmer very gently for 15 minutes. Stir in the peas, season and arrange the fish over the top. Cover with foil and continue to cook over a very low heat for 5 minutes. Serve garnished with the chopped coriander.

Fish & Bread Soup

Serves 4

INGREDIENTS

1.8 kg/4 lb mixed whole fish
225 g/8 oz unpeeled raw prawns
2.25 litres/4 pints water
150 ml/5 fl oz olive oil
2 large onions, roughly chopped
2 celery sticks, roughly chopped
1 leek, roughly chopped
1 small fennel bulb,
   roughly chopped
5 garlic cloves, chopped
1 strip of orange peel

3 tbsp orange juice
400 g/14 oz can
   chopped tomatoes
1 red pepper, deseeded
   and sliced
1 bay leaf
1 fresh thyme sprig
large pinch of saffron
large pinch of cayenne pepper
6–8 thick slices sourdough bread
salt and pepper

RED PEPPER AND
   SAFFRON SAUCE
1 red pepper, deseeded
   and quartered
150 ml/5 fl oz olive oil
1 egg yolk
large pinch of saffron
pinch of chilli flakes
lemon juice, if necessary
salt and pepper

1 Fillet the fish, reserving all the bones. Roughly chop the flesh. Peel the prawns. Place the fish bones and the prawn shells in a large saucepan with the water and bring to the boil. Simmer for 20 minutes, then strain and reserve.

2 Heat the oil in a large pan and gently fry the onions, celery, leek, fennel and garlic for 20 minutes without colouring. Add the orange peel and juice, tomatoes, red pepper, bay leaf, thyme, saffron, prawns, fish fillets and stock, bring to the boil and simmer for 40 minutes.

3 For the sauce, brush the red pepper quarters with some of the olive oil. Place under a hot preheated grill for 8–10 minutes, turning once, until the skins have blackened and the flesh is tender. Put in a plastic bag.

4 Once cool, peel off the skin. Roughly chop the flesh and place in a food

processor with the egg yolk, saffron, chilli flakes and seasoning. Blend until smooth. Add the olive oil, in a slow stream, until the sauce begins to thicken. Continue adding in a steady stream. Add seasoning to taste and lemon juice if required.

5 When the soup is cooked, process it in a food processor or blender, until smooth, then push through a sieve with a spoon. Return to the heat and season with cayenne, salt and pepper to taste. Toast the bread and place in the base of soup plates. Ladle over the soup and serve with the sauce.

Herring & Potato Pie

Serves 4

INGREDIENTS

1 tbsp Dijon mustard
115 g/4 oz butter, softened
450 g/1 lb herrings, filleted
750 g/1 lb 10 oz potatoes
1 large onion, sliced

2 cooking apples, thinly sliced
1 tsp chopped fresh sage
600 ml/1 pint hot fish stock (to
    come halfway up the sides of
    the dish)

50 g/1¾ oz crustless ciabatta
    breadcrumbs
salt and pepper
parsley sprigs, to garnish

1 Mix the Dijon mustard with 2 tablespoons of the butter until smooth. Spread this mixture over the cut sides of the herring fillets. Season to taste with salt and pepper, roll up the fillets and set them aside. Generously grease a 2 litre/4 pint pie dish with some of the remaining butter.

2 Thinly slice the potatoes, using a mandolin if possible. Blanch for 3 minutes in plenty of boiling, salted water until just tender. Drain well, refresh under cold water and pat dry.

3 Heat 2 tablespoons of the remaining butter in a frying pan and add the sliced onion. Cook over a low heat for 8–10 minutes until softened, but not coloured. Remove the pan from the heat and set aside.

4 Put half the potato slices into the bottom of the pie dish and season with salt and pepper, then add half the apples and half the onion. Put the herring fillets on top of the onion and sprinkle with the sage. Repeat the layers in reverse order, ending with potatoes. Season well and add the hot stock.

5 Melt the remaining butter and stir in the breadcrumbs until well combined. Sprinkle the breadcrumbs over the pie. Bake in a preheated oven, 190°C/375°F/Gas Mark 5, for 40–50 minutes until the breadcrumbs are golden and the herrings are cooked through. Serve garnished with parsley.

VARIATION

If herrings are unavailable, substitute mackerel or sardines.

Salt Cod Hash

Serves 4

INGREDIENTS

½ quantity Home-salted Cod
(see page 90)

4 eggs

3 tbsp olive oil, plus extra
for drizzling

8 rashers rindless smoked streaky
bacon, chopped

700 g/1 lb 9 oz old
potatoes, diced

8 garlic cloves

8 thick slices good-quality
white bread

2 plum tomatoes, peeled
and chopped

2 tsp red wine vinegar

2 tbsp chopped fresh parsley,
plus extra to garnish

salt and pepper

lemon wedges, to garnish

1 Soak the prepared cod in cold water for 2 hours. Drain well. Bring a large saucepan of water to the boil and add the fish. Remove from the heat and leave to stand for 10 minutes. Drain the fish on kitchen paper and flake the flesh. Set aside. Discard the cooking water.

2 Bring a saucepan of water to the boil and add the eggs. Simmer the eggs for 7–9 minutes from when the water returns to the boil – 7 minutes for a slightly soft centre, 9 for a firm centre.

Immediately drain, then plunge the eggs into cold water to stop them cooking further. When cool enough to handle, shell the eggs and roughly chop. Set aside.

3 Heat the oil in a large frying pan and add the bacon. Cook over a medium heat for 4–5 minutes until crisp and brown. Remove with a slotted spoon and drain on kitchen paper. Add the potatoes to the pan with the garlic and cook over a medium heat for 8–10 minutes until crisp and golden.

4 Toast the bread on both sides until golden. Drizzle with olive oil and set aside.

5 Add the plum tomatoes, bacon, fish, vinegar and reserved chopped egg to the potatoes and garlic. Cook for a further 2 minutes. Stir in the parsley and season to taste. Put the toast on serving plates, top with the hash and garnish with parsley and lemon wedges.

Pizza Marinara

Serves 4

INGREDIENTS

225 g/8 oz strong white
    bread flour

1 tsp salt

7 g/¼ oz sachet easy-blend yeast

2 tbsp olive oil, plus extra
    for oiling

150 ml/5 fl oz hand-hot water

TOMATO SAUCE

2 tbsp olive oil

1 small onion, finely chopped

1 garlic clove, crushed

400 g/14 oz can chopped
    tomatoes

1 tsp dried oregano

1 tbsp tomato purée

salt and pepper

MIXED SEAFOOD

16 live mussels, scrubbed
    and bearded

16 large clams, scrubbed

1 tbsp olive oil

12 raw tiger prawns

225 g/8 oz cleaned squid,
    cut into rings

2 x 150 g/5½ oz balls mozzarella,
    drained and sliced

olive oil, for drizzling

handful of basil leaves

salt and pepper

1 To make the pizza base, mix together the flour, salt and yeast. Add the oil and enough water to make a soft, firm dough. Turn out on to a floured surface and knead for 5 minutes until smooth and elastic.

2 Form dough into a ball and drop into an oiled bowl. Lightly oil the top of the dough, cover with a clean tea towel and leave to rise in a warm place for about 1 hour, or until doubled in bulk.

3 Meanwhile, make the sauce. Heat the oil in a pan over a medium heat and fry the onion for 5 minutes until softened. Add the garlic

and cook for 30 seconds. Add the tomatoes, oregano and tomato purée and season. Bring to the boil and simmer, uncovered, for 30 minutes until thick. Leave to cool.

4 Put the mussels and clams in a pan with only the water clinging to their shells. Cover and cook over a high heat for 3–4 minutes, shaking occasionally, until the shells have opened. Discard any that remain closed. Strain, discarding the cooking liquid. When cool, remove the seafood from their shells.

5 Heat the oil in a frying pan and fry the prawns and squid for 2–3 minutes

until the prawns have turned pink and the squid has become firm.

6 Preheat the oven to 230°C/450°F/Gas Mark 8 with baking trays on the top and middle shelves. Knock back the risen dough, divide in 2 and shape into 25 cm/ 10 inch in rounds.

7 Spread half the tomato sauce on each pizza and add the seafood. Season and top with the cheese. Drizzle with olive oil and bake for 12–15 minutes, swapping halfway through the cooking time, until golden. Serve immediately, sprinkled with the basil.

Onion & Tuna Tart

Serves 4

INGREDIENTS

225 g/8 oz strong white bread flour	TOPPING	1 tsp fresh thyme leaves
1 tsp salt	4 tbsp butter	200 g/7 oz can tuna, drained
7 g/¼ oz sachet easy-blend yeast	2 tbsp olive oil	85 g/3 oz stoned black olives
2 tbsp olive oil, plus extra for oiling	900 g/2 lb 9 oz onions, thinly sliced	pepper
150 ml/5 fl oz hand-hot water	1 tsp sugar	green salad, to serve
	1 tsp salt	

1 To make the topping, heat the butter and oil in a large saucepan and add the onions. Stir, cover and cook, over a very low heat for 20 minutes. Add the sugar and salt. Cover and cook, stirring frequently, for a further 30–40 minutes until collapsed and beginning to brown. Uncover and cook for a further 15–20 minutes until evenly golden. Remove from the heat, stir in the thyme and seasoning.

2 Meanwhile, make the base. Mix together the flour, salt and yeast in a large bowl. Add the oil and enough water to make a soft dough that leaves the sides of the bowl clean. Turn out on to a lightly floured surface and knead for 5 minutes until smooth and elastic.

3 Form the dough into a ball and drop into a lightly oiled bowl. Lightly oil the top of the dough, cover with a clean tea towel and set aside to rise in a warm place for about 1 hour, or until doubled in bulk.

4 Preheat the oven to 220°C/450°F/Gas Mark 7 with a baking tray on the top shelf. Knock back the risen dough, then turn out on to a work surface and knead briefly. Roll out the dough, using a rolling pin, to fit a lightly oiled Swiss roll tin

measuring 33 x 23 cm/13 x 9 inches, leaving a rim. You may have to stretch the dough to fit the tin as it is very springy.

5 Spread the onions in an even layer over the dough. Flake the tuna and put it on top of the onions. Arrange the olives over the tuna and season to taste with black pepper. Transfer the tin to the preheated baking tray and cook for 20 minutes until the dough is golden. Serve the tart immediately with a green salad.

Fish Pasties

Serves 4

INGREDIENTS

450 g/1 lb self-raising flour	85 g/3 oz leek, diced	4 tsp white wine vinegar
pinch of salt	85 g/3 oz onion, finely chopped	4 tbsp grated Cheddar cheese
225 g/8 oz butter, diced	85 g/3 oz carrot, diced	1 tsp chopped fresh tarragon
1 egg, lightly beaten	225 g/8 oz potato, diced	salt and pepper
	350 g/12 oz firm white fish (use	mixed salad, to serve
FILLING	the cheapest available), cut	
4 tbsp butter	into 2.5 cm/1 inch pieces	

1 Sift the flour and salt together into a bowl. Rub in the butter with your fingertips until the mixture resembles breadcrumbs. Add about 3 tablespoons cold water to form a dough. Knead briefly until smooth. Wrap in clingfilm and chill for 30 minutes.

2 To make the filling, melt half the butter in a large frying pan and add the leek, onion and carrot. Cook over a low heat for 7–8 minutes until the vegetables are softened. Remove the pan from the heat and set aside to cool slightly.

3 Put the vegetable mixture into a large mixing bowl and add the potato, fish, vinegar, remaining butter, cheese, tarragon and seasoning. Set aside.

4 Remove the pastry from the refrigerator and roll out thinly. Using a pastry cutter, stamp out 4 x 19cm/ 7½ inch discs. Alternatively, use a small plate of a similar size. Divide the filling between the 4 discs. Moisten the edges of the pastry and fold over. Pinch to seal. Crimp the edges and place the pasties on a lightly greased baking tray. Brush generously with the beaten egg, avoiding the base of the pastry to prevent the pasties sticking to the tray.

5 Bake in a preheated oven, 200°C/400°F/Gas Mark 6, for 15 minutes. Remove from the oven and brush again with the egg glaze. Return to the oven for a further 20 minutes. Serve hot or cold with a salad.

Buckwheat Pancakes with Smoked Salmon & Crème Fraîche

Serves 4

INGREDIENTS

55 g/2 oz plain flour
55 g/2 oz buckwheat flour
pinch of salt
2 large eggs
200 ml/7 fl oz milk
85 ml/3 fl oz water
2 tbsp butter, melted
vegetable oil for frying

FILLING
125 ml/4 fl oz crème fraîche
1 tbsp capers, drained, rinsed and
    roughly chopped
3 spring onions, finely chopped
1 red chilli, deseeded and
    finely chopped
1 tbsp chopped fresh dill

1 tbsp chopped fresh chives
1 tsp lemon rind
225 g /8 oz sliced smoked salmon
salt and pepper

1 For the filling, mix together the crème fraîche, capers, spring onions, red chilli, dill, chives and lemon rind, season to taste with salt and pepper and set aside.

2 To make the buckwheat pancakes, sift together the flours and salt into a large bowl. Make a well in the centre and add the eggs. Mix together the milk and water and add half this mixture to the flour and eggs. Mix together until smooth. Gradually add the remaining milk mixture until you have a smooth batter. Stir in the melted butter.

3 Heat a 20 cm/8 inch pancake pan or frying pan over a medium heat. Dip a piece of wadded kitchen paper into a little vegetable oil and rub this over the surface of the pan to give a thin coating. Ladle about 2 tablespoons pancake mixture into the pan, tilting and shaking the pan to coat the bottom evenly. Cook for 1 minute until the edges start to lift away from the pan. Using a large palette knife, carefully lift the pancake and turn it over. It should be pale golden. Cook for 30 seconds on the second side. Remove from the pan and place on a warmed plate. Re-grease and reheat the pan and repeat with the remaining mixture to make 12–14 pancakes, depending on their thickness.

4 Place a slice of smoked salmon on a pancake and top with 2 teaspoons of the crème fraîche mixture. Fold the pancake in half and then in half again to form a triangle. Repeat with the other pancakes and serve.

Entertaining

The recipes in this chapter have been designed for those occasions when you really want to make an impression. Fish and shellfish are ideal for entertaining.

They are perceived to be more exotic than many meat dishes and yet are often easier to prepare. Shellfish, in particular, is thought to be luxurious, but nowadays it is readily available and reasonably priced.

There should be something here for every budget, ability and taste, from Stuffed Monkfish Tail and Crab Soufflé to Hot-smoked Trout Tart and Spinach Roulade.

There are more traditional dishes, such as Luxury Fish Pie and Sole Florentine, as well as more exciting dishes like Cuttlefish in their own Ink.

Skate with Black Butter

Serves 4

INGREDIENTS

900 g/2 lb skate wings, cut into 4
175 g/6 oz butter
50 ml/2 fl oz red wine vinegar
1 tbsp capers, drained and rinsed
1 tbsp chopped fresh parsley
fresh parsley sprigs, to garnish

COURT-BOUILLON
850 ml/1½ pints water
850 ml/1½ pints dry white wine
3 tbsp white wine vinegar
2 large carrots, roughly chopped
1 onion, roughly chopped
2 celery sticks, roughly chopped
2 leeks, roughly chopped
2 garlic cloves, roughly chopped

2 fresh bay leaves
4 parsley sprigs
4 thyme sprigs
6 black peppercorns
1 tsp salt

TO SERVE
new potatoes
green beans

1 Begin by making the court-bouillon. Put all of the ingredients into a large saucepan and bring to the boil over a low heat. Cover and simmer gently for 30 minutes. Strain the liquid through a fine sieve into a clean pan. Discard the flavourings. Bring to the boil again and boil, uncovered, for 15–20 minutes, until reduced to 600 ml/1 pint.

2 Place the skate in a wide shallow pan and pour in the court-bouillon. Bring to the boil and simmer very gently for 15–20 minutes, depending on the thickness of the skate. Drain the fish, set aside on serving plates and keep warm.

3 Meanwhile, melt the butter in a frying pan. Cook over a medium heat until the butter changes colour to a dark brown and smells very nutty.

4 Stir in the vinegar, capers and parsley and cook over a low heat for 1 minute. Pour the butter over the fish and garnish with fresh parsley sprigs. Serve immediately with plenty of boiled new potatoes and green beans.

Dover Sole à la Meunière

Serves 4

INGREDIENTS

50 g/1¾ oz plain flour
1 tsp salt
4 x 400 g/14 oz Dover soles,
    cleaned and skinned

150 g/5½ oz butter
3 tbsp lemon juice
1 tbsp chopped fresh parsley

¼ preserved lemon, finely
    chopped (optional)
lemon wedges, to garnish

1 Mix the flour with the salt and place on a large plate or tray. Drop the fish into the flour, one at a time, and shake well to remove any excess. Melt 3 tablespoons of the butter in a small saucepan over a low heat and brush the fish all over with it.

2 Place the fish under a preheated hot grill and cook for 5 minutes each side.

3 Meanwhile, melt the remaining butter in pan. Pour cold water into a bowl, large enough to take the base of the pan. Keep nearby.

4 Gently heat the butter until it turns a golden brown colour and begins to smell nutty. Immediately remove the pan from the heat and immerse the base in the cold water to prevent any further cooking.

5 Put the grilled Dover soles on to warm individual serving plates, drizzle with the lemon juice and sprinkle with the parsley and preserved lemon, if using. Pour the hot browned butter over it and serve immediately, garnished with lemon wedges.

COOK'S TIP

If you have a large enough pan (or two) you can fry the floured fish in butter, if you prefer.

Sole Florentine

Serves 4

INGREDIENTS

600 ml/1 pint milk
2 strips lemon rind
2 fresh tarragon sprigs
1 fresh bay leaf
½ onion, sliced
2 tbsp butter, plus extra
   for greasing
50 g/1¾ oz plain flour

2 tsp mustard powder
5 tbsp freshly grated
   Parmesan cheese
300 ml/10 fl oz double cream
pinch of freshly grated nutmeg
450 g/1 lb fresh spinach, washed

4 x 750 g/1 lb 10 oz Dover sole,
   quarter-cut fillets (2 from
   each side of the fish)
salt and pepper

TO SERVE
crisp green salad
crusty bread

1 Put the milk, lemon rind, tarragon, bay leaf and onion into a saucepan and bring to the boil over a low heat. Remove the pan from the heat and set aside for 30 minutes for the flavours to infuse.

2 Melt the butter in a clean saucepan and stir in the flour and mustard powder until smooth. Strain the infused milk, discarding the lemon, herbs and onion. Gradually beat the milk into the butter and flour until

smooth. Bring to the boil over a low heat, stirring constantly, until thickened. Simmer gently for 2 minutes. Remove from the heat and stir in the cheese, double cream and nutmeg. Season to taste with salt and pepper. Cover the surface of the sauce with baking paper or clingfilm and set aside.

3 Lightly grease a large ovenproof dish. Blanch the spinach leaves in plenty of boiling salted water for 30 seconds. Drain and

immediately refresh under cold water. Drain and pat dry. Put the spinach in a layer on the bottom of the greased dish.

4 Wash and dry the fish fillets. Season and roll up. Arrange on top of the spinach and pour over the cheese sauce. Transfer to a preheated oven, 200°C/ 400°F/Gas Mark 6, and cook for 35 minutes until bubbling and golden. Serve immediately with a crisp green salad and crusty bread.

VARIATION

For a budget version of this dish, use lemon sole instead of Dover sole.

John Dory en Papillote

Serves 4

INGREDIENTS

2 John Dory, filleted
115 g/4 oz stoned black olives
12 cherry tomatoes, halved
115 g/4 oz green beans, trimmed

handful fresh basil leaves
4 lemon slices
4 tsp olive oil
salt and pepper

fresh basil leaves, to garnish
boiled new potatoes, to serve

1 Wash the fish fillets, pat dry with kitchen paper and set aside. Cut 4 large rectangles of baking paper measuring 45 x 30 cm/ 18 x 12 inches. Fold each one in half to give a 23 x 30 cm/ 9 x 12 inch rectangle. Cut these into large heart shapes and open out.

2 Lay 1 John Dory fillet on one half of the paper heart. Top with a quarter of the olives, tomatoes, green beans and basil leaves. Add 1 lemon slice. Drizzle over 1 teaspoon of the olive oil and season to taste with salt and pepper.

3 Fold over the other half of the paper and fold the edges of the paper together to enclose. Repeat to make 4 parcels.

4 Place the parcels on a baking tray and cook in a preheated oven, 200°C/ 400°F/Gas Mark 6, for about 15 minutes or until the fish is tender and cooked through.

5 Transfer each parcel, unopened, to a serving plate, allowing your guests to open their parcels and enjoy the wonderful aroma. Suggest that they garnish their portions with fresh basil leaves and serve with boiled new potatoes.

VARIATION

Try spreading the fish with a little olive paste, some chopped sun-dried tomatoes, a little goat's cheese and fresh basil.

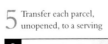

Grilled Sea Bass with Stewed Artichokes

Serves 4

INGREDIENTS

1.8 kg/4 lb baby artichokes

7½ tsp fresh lemon juice, plus the cut halves of the lemon

175 ml/6 fl oz olive oil

10 garlic cloves, thinly sliced

1 tbsp fresh thyme plus extra, to garnish

6 x 115 g/4 oz sea bass fillets

salt and pepper

crusty bread, to serve

1 Peel away the tough outer leaves of each artichoke until the yellow-green heart is revealed. Slice off the pointed top at about halfway between the point and the top of the stem. Cut off the stem and pare off what is left of the dark green leaves surrounding the bottom of the artichoke.

2 Submerge the prepared artichokes in water containing the cut halves of the lemon to prevent them from browning. When all the artichokes have been prepared, place them, choke side down, and slice thinly.

3 Heat 175 ml/5 fl oz of the olive oil in a large, heavy-based saucepan and add the sliced artichokes, garlic, thyme and lemon juice. Season to taste with salt and pepper. Cover and cook the artichokes over a low heat for 20–30 minutes, without colouring, until tender.

4 Meanwhile, brush the sea bass fillets with the remaining olive oil and season well with salt and pepper. Cook on a preheated ridged grill pan or barbecue for 3–4 minutes on each side until just tender.

5 Divide the stewed artichokes between warmed individual serving plates and top each with a sea bass fillet. Garnish with chopped thyme and serve immediately with lots of crusty bread.

VARIATION

Artichokes cooked this way also suit cod, halibut and salmon.

Sea Bass with Ratatouille

Serves 4

INGREDIENTS

2 large sea bass, filleted
olive oil, for brushing
salt and pepper

RATATOUILLE
1 large aubergine
2 medium courgettes
1 tbsp sea salt
4 tbsp olive oil

1 medium onion,
   roughly chopped
2 garlic cloves, crushed
½ red pepper, deseeded and
   roughly chopped
½ green pepper, deseeded and
   roughly chopped
2 large ripe tomatoes, peeled and
   chopped

1 tbsp chopped fresh basil
salt and pepper

DRESSING
5 tbsp roughly chopped
   fresh basil
2 garlic cloves, roughly chopped
4 tbsp olive oil
1 tbsp lemon juice
salt and pepper

1 To make the ratatouille, cut the aubergine and courgettes into chunks about the same size as the onion and peppers. Put the aubergine and courgettes in a colander with the salt and set aside to drain for about 30 minutes. Rinse well under cold running water and pat dry on kitchen paper.

2 Heat the oil in a large saucepan and add the onion and garlic. Cook over a low heat for 10 minutes until softened. Add the peppers, aubergine and courgettes. Season and stir well. Cover and simmer very gently for 30 minutes until all the vegetables have softened. Add the tomatoes and cook for a further 15 minutes.

3 Meanwhile make the dressing. Put the basil, garlic, and half the olive oil into a food processor and process until finely chopped. Add the remaining olive oil, lemon juice and seasoning.

4 Season the sea bass fillets and brush with a little oil. Preheat a frying pan until very hot and add the fish, skin side down. Cook for 2–3 minutes until the skin is browned and crispy. Turn the fish and cook for a further 2–3 minutes until just cooked through.

5 To serve, stir the basil into the ratatouille, then divide between 4 serving plates. Top with the fried fish and spoon the dressing around them.

Whole Sea Bass with Ginger & Spring Onions

Serves 4

INGREDIENTS

800 g/1 lb 12 oz sea bass,
   cleaned and scaled
4 tbsp light soy sauce
5 spring onions, cut into long,
   fine shreds

2 tbsp finely shredded fresh
   root ginger
4 tbsp fresh coriander leaves
5 tsp sunflower oil

1 tsp sesame oil
4 tbsp hot fish stock
lime wedges, to garnish
steamed rice, to serve

1 Wash the fish inside and out under cold running water and pat dry with kitchen paper. Brush with 2 tablespoons of the soy sauce. Scatter half the spring onions and all the ginger over a steaming tray or large plate and put the fish on top.

2 Half fill a large saucepan with water and fit a steamer on top. Bring the water to the boil. Put the steaming plate with the sea bass into the steamer and cover with a tight-fitting lid. Keeping the water in the pan boiling, steam the fish for 10–12 minutes until tender.

3 Carefully remove the plate from the steamer and lift the fish on to a warm serving platter, leaving the spring onions and ginger behind on the steaming plate. Scatter the remaining spring onions and the coriander leaves over the fish.

4 Put the sunflower oil into a small saucepan and heat until almost smoking. Add the sesame oil and immediately pour the mixture over the fish and spring onions.

5 Mix the remaining soy sauce with the hot fish stock and pour this mixture over the fish. Serve the sea bass immediately with steamed rice and garnished with lime wedges.

Cold Poached Cod Steaks with a Pickled Vegetable Relish

Serves 4

INGREDIENTS

1 small carrot, thinly sliced
1 small onion, thinly sliced
1 celery stick, thinly sliced
3 fresh parsley sprigs
3 fresh thyme sprigs
1 garlic clove, sliced
1.7 litres/3 pints water
1 tsp salt
4 x 175 g/6 oz cod steaks
dressed salad leaves, to serve

PICKLED VEGETABLE RELISH
1 small carrot, finely diced
¼ red pepper, deseeded and
    finely diced
½ small red onion, finely diced
1 garlic clove, finely chopped
3 tbsp finely diced
    cornichon pickles
4 tbsp chopped stoned
    green olives

1 tbsp capers, drained and rinsed
2 salted anchovies, soaked in
    several changes of water for
    15 minutes, chopped
1 tbsp red wine vinegar
100 ml/3½ fl oz olive oil
2 tbsp chopped fresh parsley
salt and pepper

1 Put the carrot, onion, celery, parsley, thyme, garlic, water and salt into a large saucepan. Bring to the boil and simmer over a low heat for 10 minutes.

2 Add the cod steaks and poach for 5–7 minutes until just firm in the centre. Remove the fish with a perforated spoon and leave to cool. Refrigerate for 2 hours.

3 Meanwhile, make the pickled vegetable relish. Combine the carrot, red pepper, red onion, garlic, cornichons, olives, capers, anchovies, vinegar, olive oil and parsley in a non-metallic bowl. Season to taste with salt and pepper and add a little more vinegar or olive oil if desired. Cover with clingfilm and chill in the refrigerator for 1 hour.

4 To serve, place a cold cod steak on each of 4 serving plates. Spoon the relish over the top. Serve with dressed salad leaves.

Sea Bream in a Salt Crust

Serves 4

INGREDIENTS

1 kg/2 lb 4 oz sea bream
1 shallot, thinly sliced
2 fresh parsley sprigs
1 fresh tarragon sprig
2 garlic cloves, roughly chopped
2–2.5 kg/4 lb 8 oz–5 lb 8 oz
    coarse sea salt

LEMON BUTTER SAUCE
2 shallots, very finely chopped
4 tbsp lemon juice
300 g/10½ oz cold unsalted
    butter, diced
salt and pepper

TO GARNISH
lemon wedges
fresh herbs

1 Wash the sea bream inside and out under cold running water and pat dry with kitchen paper. Stuff the body cavity with the shallot, parsley, tarragon and garlic. Set aside.

2 Sprinkle a thick layer of sea salt into the bottom of a roasting tin large enough to hold the fish with lots of space around it. Place the fish on top, then pour the remaining salt over the fish to cover it completely. Sprinkle the water lightly all over the salt. Cook in a preheated

oven, 220°C/425°F/Gas Mark 7, for 25 minutes.

3 Meanwhile, make the lemon butter sauce. Put the shallots and lemon juice into a saucepan and simmer gently for 5 minutes. Increase the heat and boil until the lemon juice is reduced by half. Reduce the heat to low and add the butter, 1 piece at a time, whisking constantly, until all the butter has been fully incorporated and the sauce is thickened. Season to taste with salt and pepper and keep warm.

4 Remove the fish from the oven and allow to stand for 5 minutes before cracking open the salt. Remove the fish, garnish with lemon wedges and fresh herbs and serve with the lemon butter sauce.

COOK'S TIP

The salt keeps the fish wonderfully moist and tender, but brush away all traces of the crust before serving.

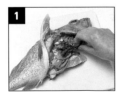

Cuttlefish in their own Ink

Serves 4

INGREDIENTS

450 g/1 lb small cuttlefish, with
    their ink (or substitute squid)
4 tbsp olive oil
1 small onion, finely chopped
2 garlic cloves, finely chopped

1 tsp paprika, preferably Spanish
175 g/6 oz ripe tomatoes, peeled,
    deseeded and chopped
150 ml/5 fl oz red wine
150 ml/5 fl oz fish stock

225 g/8 oz instant polenta
3 tbsp chopped fresh
    flat-leaved parsley
salt and pepper

1 To prepare the cuttlefish, cut off the tentacles in front of the eyes and remove the beak-like mouth from the centre of the tentacles. Cut the head section from the body and discard it. Cut open the body section from top to bottom along the dark coloured back. Remove the cuttle bone and the entrails, reserving the ink sac. Skin the body, rinse in cold water and pat dry. Chop the flesh roughly and set aside. Split open the ink sac and dilute the ink in a little water in a small bowl. Set aside.

2 Heat the oil in a large saucepan and add the onion. Cook over a low heat for 8–10 minutes until softened and starting to brown. Add the garlic and cook for a further 30 seconds. Add the cuttlefish and cook for a further 5 minutes until starting to brown. Add the paprika and stir for a further 30 seconds before adding the tomatoes. Cook for a further 2–3 minutes until collapsed.

3 Add the red wine, fish stock and diluted cuttlefish ink and stir well.

Bring to the boil and simmer gently, uncovered, for 25 minutes until the cuttlefish is tender and the sauce has thickened. Season to taste with salt and pepper.

4 Meanwhile, cook the polenta according to the packet instructions. When cooked, remove from the heat and stir in the parsley and seasoning.

5 Divide the polenta between 4 serving plates and top with the cuttlefish and its sauce.

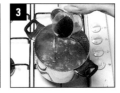

Noisettes of Salmon

Serves 4

INGREDIENTS

4 salmon steaks
2 tbsp vegetable oil
4 tbsp butter, softened
1 garlic clove, crushed
2 tsp mustard seeds

2 tbsp chopped fresh thyme
1 tbsp chopped fresh parsley
4 tomatoes, peeled, deseeded
   and chopped
salt and pepper

TO SERVE
new potatoes
green vegetables or salad

1 Carefully remove the central bone from the salmon steaks and cut the steaks in half. Curl each piece around to form a medallion and tie with string.

2 Heat the oil in a ridged pan or frying pan. Add the salmon noisettes, in batches if necessary, and fry on both sides to brown. Remove from the pan, drain on kitchen paper and set aside to cool.

3 Beat together the butter, garlic, mustard, thyme and parsley until fully incorporated. Season to taste with salt and pepper.

4 Cut 4 pieces of baking paper into 30 cm/12 inch squares. Place 2 salmon noisettes on top of each square and top with a little of the flavoured butter and a quarter of the tomatoes. Draw up the edges of the paper and fold together to enclose the fish. Place on a baking tray.

5 Cook in a preheated oven, 200°C/400°F/Gas Mark 6, for 10–15 minutes or until the salmon is cooked through. Remove the noisettes from the parcels and transfer to warmed serving plates. Remove and discard the string. Serve immediately, while still warm, with new potatoes and green vegetables or a salad.

VARIATION

You can make cod steaks into noisettes in the same way. Cook them with butter flavoured with chives and basil.

Whole Poached Salmon

Serves 4–6

INGREDIENTS

1.5 kg/3 lb 5 oz salmon, cleaned and scaled	WATERCRESS MAYONNAISE	50 g/1¾ oz watercress leaves, roughly chopped
3 x quantity Court-bouillon (see page 122)	1 egg yolk	225 ml/8 fl oz/ light olive oil
½ cucumber, very thinly sliced	1 garlic clove, crushed	1 spring onion, finely chopped
	1 tsp Dijon mustard	salt and pepper
	1 tbsp lemon juice	
	1 tbsp chopped fresh basil	

1 Wash and dry the salmon and remove the fins. Place the salmon in a fish kettle or large, heavy-based roasting tin. Pour over the Court-bouillon. Bring to the boil over a low heat and, as soon as the liquid comes to a simmer, remove from the heat and leave to go cold.

2 Meanwhile, make the watercress mayonnaise. Put the egg yolk, garlic, mustard, lemon juice, basil and watercress into a food processor and process until the herbs are very finely chopped. Begin adding the olive oil, drop by drop, until the mixture begins to thicken. Then add the olive oil in a steady stream until it is all incorporated. Scrape the mayonnaise into a bowl and add the spring onion. Season to taste with salt and pepper. Cover with clingfilm and refrigerate until needed.

3 When the salmon is cold, carefully lift it from the poaching liquid and pat dry with kitchen paper. Carefully peel away and discard the skin from the rounder, uppermost side, then carefully turn the fish and remove the skin from the flatter, underside. Carefully slide a large knife along the backbone of the fish to remove the flesh in one piece. Turn it over on to your serving platter so that the cut side is up.

4 Remove the bones from the remaining piece of fish. Finally, turn the remaining flesh on top of the first piece to reform the fish. This makes serving much easier. Place the head and tail back on the fish to make it appear whole.

5 Lay the cucumber slices on top of the fish, starting at the tail end, in a pattern resembling scales. Serve with the mayonnaise.

Stuffed Monkfish Tail

Serves 6

INGREDIENTS

750 g/1 lb 10 oz monkfish tail,
  skinned and trimmed
6 slices Parma ham
4 tbsp chopped mixed herbs such
  as parsley, chives, basil, sage

1 tsp finely grated lemon rind
2 tbsp olive oil
salt and pepper

TO SERVE
shredded stir-fried vegetables
new potatoes

1 Using a sharp knife, carefully cut down each side of the central bone of the monkfish to leave 2 fillets. Wash the fillets under cold running water and pat dry with kitchen paper.

2 Lay the Parma ham slices widthways on a clean work surface so that they overlap slightly. Lay the fish fillets lengthways on top of the ham so that the two cut sides face each other.

3 Mix together the chopped herbs and lemon rind. Season well with salt and pepper. Pack this mixture on to the cut surface of one monkfish fillet. Press the 2 fillets together and wrap tightly with the Parma ham slices. Secure with string or cocktail sticks.

4 Heat the olive oil in a large ovenproof frying pan and place the fish in the pan, seam side down first, and brown the wrapped monkfish tail all over.

5 Cook in a preheated oven, 200°C/400°F/Gas Mark 6, for 25 minutes until golden and the fish is tender.

Remove from the oven and allow to rest for 10 minutes before slicing thickly. Serve with shredded stir-fried vegetables and new potatoes.

COOK'S TIP

It is possible to remove the central bone from a monkfish tail without separating the two fillets completely. This makes it easier to stuff, but takes some practice.

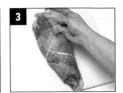

Grilled Lobster with Beurre Blanc

Serves 4

INGREDIENTS

4 x 450 g/1lb live lobsters	1 tbsp white wine vinegar	1 tbsp chopped fresh parsley
2 tbsp butter	1 tbsp dry white wine	Salt and pepper
	50 ml/2 fl oz water	
BEURRE BLANC	150 g/5½ oz cold unsalted	TO GARNISH
25 g/1 oz shallots,	butter, diced	lemon wedges
finely chopped	2 tsp chopped fresh tarragon	fresh herb sprigs

1 Put the lobsters into the freezer for about 2 hours, then take a very large knife and cleave them in two, lengthways behind the head. Dot the lobster flesh with the butter. Transfer to a grill pan and cook, flesh side up, under a preheated very hot grill for 5–7 minutes until the flesh of the lobster becomes firm and opaque.

2 Meanwhile, put the shallots into a small saucepan with the vinegar, white wine and water. Bring to the boil and simmer until only 1 tablespoon of liquid remains. Reduce the heat to low and begin adding the butter, one piece at a time, whisking constantly. Only add the next piece of butter when the last piece has been fully incorporated and continue until all the butter has been used and the sauce has thickened. Remove the pan from the heat.

3 Stir in the tarragon and parsley and season to taste with salt and pepper.

4 Transfer the lobster to 4 serving plates and spoon over the beurre blanc.

Garnish with lemon wedges and fresh herbs.

COOK'S TIP

The RSPCA has suggested that putting the lobsters in a freezer for 2 hours before cooking them will kill them painlessly but, if you are squeamish about such things, ask the fishmonger to do it for you.

Lobster & Avocado Salad

Serves 4

INGREDIENTS

2 x 400 g/14 oz cooked lobsters
1 large avocado
1 tbsp lemon juice
225 g/8 oz green beans

4 spring onions, thinly sliced
2 tbsp chopped fresh chervil
1 tbsp chopped fresh chives
salt

DRESSING
1 garlic clove, crushed
1 tsp Dijon mustard
pinch of sugar
1 tbsp balsamic vinegar
5 tbsp olive oil
salt and pepper

1 To prepare the lobsters, cut them in half lengthways. Remove the intestinal vein which runs down the tail, the stomach sac and any grey beards from the body cavity at the head end of the lobster. Crack the claws and remove the meat – in one piece if possible. Remove the meat from the tail of the lobster. Roughly chop all the meat and set aside.

2 Split the avocado lengthways and remove the stone. Cut each half in half again and peel away the skin. Cut the avocado into chunks and toss with the lemon juice. Add to the lobster meat.

3 Bring a large pan of lightly salted water to the boil and add the beans. Cook for 3 minutes, then drain and immediately refresh under cold water. Drain again and leave to go completely cold. Cut the beans in half then mix well with the avocado and lobster.

4 Meanwhile, make the dressing by whisking together the garlic, mustard, sugar and vinegar. Season to taste with salt and pepper. Gradually add the oil, whisking, until thickened.

5 Add the spring onions, chervil and chives to the lobster and avocado mixture and toss gently together. Drizzle over the dressing and serve immediately.

Platter de Fruit de Mers

Serves 4

INGREDIENTS

36 live mussels, scrubbed and bearded	SHALLOT VINAIGRETTE	1 tbsp lemon juice
clams, cockles, winkles, whelks scallops and sea urchins	150 ml/5 fl oz red wine vinegar	300 ml/10 fl oz olive oil
	3 shallots, finely chopped	salt and pepper
18 live oysters	1 tbsp olive oil	
3 x 450 g/1 lb cooked lobsters	salt and pepper	TO SERVE
3 x 750 g/1 lb 10 oz cooked crabs		seaweed
36 cooked langoustines or prawns	MAYONNAISE	crushed ice
	1 egg yolk	3 lemons, cut into wedges
	1 tsp Dijon mustard	

1 First prepare the seafood of your choice. Steam mussels, clams and cockles with just the water on their shells after washing for about 3–4 minutes until just open. Drain and refresh under cold water. Put winkles and whelks in separate pans of lightly salted boiling water. Drain the winkles as soon as the water returns to the boil. Simmer the whelks for 4 minutes, then drain. Steam scallops on the half shell until the flesh just turns white. Cut sea urchins in half and drain off any excess water. Put oysters into a pan with a just splash of water. Cook over a high heat for 3–4 minutes, drain and refresh under cold water.

2 For the vinaigrette, mix together the vinegar, shallots and olive oil and season to taste with salt and pepper. Leave at room temperature for 2 hours.

3 For the mayonnaise, put the egg yolk, mustard, lemon juice and salt and pepper to taste into a food processor and process for 30 seconds until foaming. With the motor running, add the oil, drop by drop, until the mixture begins to thicken. Then add the oil in a steady stream until all of it is incorporated. Add a little hot water if the mixture is too thick. Cover and refrigerate.

4 To assemble, place the seaweed on a platter and top with the ice. Arrange the seafood with the lemon wedges on top, scattering on more crushed ice as you go. Serve the mayonnaise and shallot vinaigrette separately.

Bouillabaisse

Serves 6–8

INGREDIENTS

5 tbsp olive oil
2 large onions, finely chopped
1 leek, finely chopped
4 garlic cloves, crushed
½ small fennel bulb,
    finely chopped
5 ripe tomatoes, peeled
    and chopped
1 fresh thyme sprig
2 strips of orange rind

1.7 litres/3 pints hot fish stock
2 kg/4 lb 8oz mixed fish, such as
    John Dory, sea bass, sea
    bream, red mullet, cod, skate,
    soft-shell crabs, raw prawns,
    langoustines, roughly
    chopped into equal-size
    pieces (shellfish left whole)
12–18 thick slices French bread
salt and pepper

RED PEPPER AND
    SAFFRON SAUCE
1 red pepper, deseeded and cut
    into quarters
150 ml/5 fl oz light olive oil
1 egg yolk
large pinch of saffron
pinch of chilli flakes
lemon juice, to taste
salt and pepper

1 First, make the red pepper and saffron sauce. Brush the red pepper quarters with a little of the oil. Cook under a preheated grill for 5–6 minutes on each side until charred. Place in a plastic bag until cool enough to handle. Peel off the skins.

2 Place the pepper pieces, egg yolk, saffron, chilli flakes, lemon juice and salt and pepper to taste in a food processor. Process until smooth. With the motor running, add the remaining oil, drop by drop, until the mixture begins to thicken. Then add it in a steady stream until incorporated and the mixture is thick. Add a little hot water if it is too thick.

3 Heat the olive oil in a large pan and fry the onions, leek, garlic and fennel for 10–15 minutes until softened and starting to colour. Add the tomatoes, thyme, orange rind and seasoning and fry for a further 5 minutes until the tomatoes have collapsed.

4 Add the stock and bring to the boil. Simmer for 10 minutes until all the vegetables are tender. Add the fish and return to the boil. Simmer gently for 10 minutes until tender.

5 Toast the bread. Spoon the fish on to serving plates. Add some of the soup to moisten it and serve with the bread and red pepper and saffron sauce. Serve the remaining soup separately.

Crab Soufflé

Serves 4–6

INGREDIENTS

3 tbsp butter, plus extra
for greasing
25 g/1 oz dried breadcrumbs
1 small onion, finely chopped
1 garlic clove, crushed
2 tsp mustard powder

25 g/1 oz plain flour
225 ml/8 fl oz milk
50 g/1¾ oz Gruyère
cheese, grated
3 eggs, separated

225 g/8 oz fresh crab meat,
defrosted if frozen
2 tbsp chopped fresh chives
pinch of cayenne pepper
salt and pepper

1 Generously butter a 1.5 litre/2½ pint soufflé dish. Add the breadcrumbs and shake around the dish to coat completely, shaking out any excess. Set aside on a baking tray.

2 Melt the butter in a large pan. Add the onion and cook over a low heat, stirring occasionally, for 8 minutes until softened but not coloured. Add the garlic and cook for a further minute.

3 Stir in the mustard powder and flour and cook, stirring, for 1 minute.

Gradually add the milk, stirring constantly, until smooth. Increase the heat slightly and bring slowly to the boil, stirring constantly. Simmer gently for 2 minutes. Remove the pan from the heat and stir in the cheese. Leave to cool slightly.

4 Lightly beat in the egg yolks, then fold in the crab meat, chives and cayenne and season to taste with salt and pepper.

5 In a clean bowl, whisk the egg whites until they form stiff peaks. Add a large

spoonful of the egg whites to the crab mixture and fold together to slacken. Add the remaining egg whites and fold together carefully, but thoroughly. Spoon into the prepared dish.

6 Cook in a preheated oven, 200°C/400°F/Gas Mark 6, for 25 minutes until well risen and golden. Serve immediately.

Spinach Roulade

Serves 4

INGREDIENTS

2 tbsp butter, plus extra
    for greasing
225 g/8 oz frozen spinach,
    thawed and well drained
4 tbsp plain flour
200 ml/7 fl oz milk
4 eggs, separated
1 tbsp chopped fresh tarragon

½ tsp freshly grated nutmeg
salt and pepper

FILLING
375 g/12 oz skinless smoked
    cod fillet
115 g/4 oz ricotta cheese
4 tbsp grated Parmesan cheese

4 spring onions, finely chopped
2 tbsp chopped fresh chives
50 g/1¾ oz sun-dried tomatoes
    in olive oil, drained and
    finely chopped
salt and pepper

---

1 Grease a 33 x 23 cm/
13 x 9 inch Swiss roll tin
and line with baking paper.
Squeeze the spinach to remove
as much liquid as possible.
Chop finely and set aside.

2 Melt the butter in a
saucepan, add the flour
and cook for 30 seconds,
stirring. Gradually add the
milk, stirring constantly until
smooth. Bring slowly to
the boil and simmer for
2 minutes, stirring. Remove
from the heat and allow to
cool slightly.

3 Stir in the spinach, egg
yolks, tarragon, nutmeg
and seasoning. Whisk the egg
whites until they form stiff
peaks. Fold a large spoonful
into the spinach mixture to
slacken it, then fold in the
remaining egg whites
carefully, but thoroughly to
avoid losing any volume.
Pour the mixture into the tin
and smooth the surface.

4 Cook in a preheated
oven, 200°C/400°F/Gas
Mark 6, for 15 minutes until
risen and golden and firm in

the centre. Turn out
immediately on to a clean tea
towel, peel off the baking
paper and roll up from one
short end.

5 For the filling, cover
the cod with boiling
water and set aside for
10 minutes until just tender.
Remove the fish and flake
carefully, removing any
bones, then mix with the
ricotta, Parmesan, spring
onions, chives, sun-dried
tomatoes and seasoning.

6 Unroll the roulade and
spread with the cod
mixture, leaving a 2.5 cm/
1 inch border all around.
Tightly re-roll the roulade
and return to the oven, seam
side down, for 20 minutes.
Serve immediately.

Luxury Fish Pie

Serves 4

INGREDIENTS

85 g/3 oz butter
3 shallots, finely chopped
115 g/4 oz button
    mushrooms, halved
2 tbsp dry white wine
900 g/2 lb live mussels,
    scrubbed and bearded
300 g/10½ oz monkfish
    fillet, cubed

300 g/10½ oz skinless cod
    fillet, cubed
1 quantity Court-bouillon
    (see page 122)
300 g/10½ oz skinless lemon
    sole fillet, cubed
115 g/4 oz tiger prawns, peeled
4 tbsp plain flour
4 tbsp double cream

POTATO TOPPING
1.5 kg/3 lb 5oz floury potatoes,
    cut into chunks
4 tbsp butter
2 egg yolks
125 ml/4 fl oz milk
pinch of freshly grated nutmeg
salt and pepper
fresh parsley, to garnish

1 For the filling, melt 25 g/1 oz of the butter in a frying pan, add the shallots and cook for 5 minutes. Add the mushrooms and cook for 2 minutes. Add the wine and simmer until the liquid has evaporated. Transfer to a 1.5 litre/2¾ pint shallow ovenproof dish and set aside.

2 Put the mussels into a large saucepan with just the water clinging to their shells and cook, covered,

over a high heat for 3–4 minutes until all have opened. Discard any that remain closed. Drain, reserving the cooking liquid. When cool enough to handle, remove the mussels from their shells and add to the mushrooms.

3 Boil the Court-bouillon and add the monkfish. Poach for 2 minutes. Add the cod, sole and prawns, poach 2 minutes. Add the fish to the mussels and mushrooms.

4 Melt the remaining butter in a saucepan and add the flour. Stir until smooth and cook for 2 minutes. Gradually, stir in the hot Court-bouillon and mussel cooking liquid until smooth and thickened.

Add the cream and simmer gently for 15 minutes, stirring. Season to taste and pour over the fish.

5 Boil the potatoes, drain well and mash with the butter, egg yolks, milk, nutmeg and seasoning. Pipe over the fish, or spread with a spatula, and roughen the surface of the topping with a fork.

6 Bake the finished fish pie in a preheated oven at 200°C/ 400°F/Gas Mark 6, for 30 minutes until golden and bubbling. Serve straight from the oven, piping hot garnished with fresh parsley.

Salmon Coulibiac

Serves 4

INGREDIENTS

50 g/1¾ oz long-grain rice
3 eggs
2 tbsp vegetable oil
1 onion, finely chopped
1 garlic clove, crushed
1 tsp finely grated lemon rind
2 tbsp chopped fresh parsley

1 tbsp chopped fresh dill
450 g/1 lb salmon fillet, skinned
 and cubed
500 g/1 lb 2 oz puff pastry,
 defrosted if frozen
beaten egg, to glaze
salt

QUICK HOLLANDAISE SAUCE
175 g/6 oz butter
1 tbsp wine vinegar
2 tbsp lemon juice
3 egg yolks
salt and pepper

1 Cook the rice in lightly salted boiling water for 10–15 minutes until tender. Drain and set aside. Bring a small pan of water to the boil and add the eggs. Cook for 8 minutes from when the water returns to the boil. Drain, refresh under cold water, shell and slice thinly.

2 Heat the oil in a frying pan and cook the onion for 5 minutes until softened. Add the garlic and cook for a further 30 seconds. Add to the rice with the lemon rind, parsley, dill and salmon.

3 Roll out the pastry to a 40 x 30 cm/16 x 12 inch rectangle. Lift it on to a lightly greased baking tray. Spoon half the filling over half the pastry, leaving a border of about 2 cm/¾ inch. Top with the sliced eggs, then the remaining filling.

4 Dampen the edges of the pastry with a little beaten egg, then fold over the remaining pastry. Crimp the edges to seal well. Mark the pastry using a small sharp knife, taking care not to cut right through the pastry. Decorate with the pastry trimmings and brush with beaten egg to glaze.

5 Bake in a preheated oven, 200°C/400°F/Gas Mark 6, for 30–35 minutes until is risen and golden.

6 For the sauce, put the butter into a small saucepan and melt over a low heat. Put the wine vinegar and lemon juice into another saucepan and bring to the boil. Meanwhile, put the egg yolks and a pinch of salt in a food processor or blender and blend together. With the motor still running, gradually add the hot vinegar and lemon juice. When the butter starts to boil, start to pour this into the machine in a steady stream until all the butter has been added and the sauce has thickened. Season to taste with salt and pepper.

7 Keep the sauce warm by placing in a bowl over hot water until ready to serve. Serve the pie with a little hollandaise sauce.

Salmon & Courgette Pie

Serves 4

INGREDIENTS

2 tbsp olive oil
2 red peppers, cored, deseeded
    and chopped
1 medium onion, finely chopped
2 eggs

225 g/8 oz salmon fillet, skinned
    and cubed
1 courgette, sliced
1 tsp chopped fresh dill
salt and pepper
Chinese garlic, to garnish

PASTRY
350 g/12 oz plain flour
½ tsp salt
175 g/6 oz cold butter, diced
2 egg yolks
beaten egg or milk, to glaze

1 Heat the oil in a saucepan, add the peppers, onion and a little seasoning and cook gently for 10–15 minutes until softened. Transfer to a food processor or blender and blend until smooth or press through a fine sieve.

2 Bring a small saucepan of water to the boil. Add the eggs, cook for 10 minutes from when the water returns to the boil, then refresh immediately under cold water. When cool enough to handle, drain and shell.

3 Roughly chop the eggs and add to the pepper purée with the salmon, courgette, dill and seasoning. Mix well and set aside.

4 For the pastry, put the flour in a bowl with ½ teaspoon salt. Rub in butter and with your fingertips until the mixture resembles fine breadcrumbs. Add the egg yolks with enough cold water, about 3–4 tablespoons, to make a firm dough. Turn on to a lightly floured work surface and knead briefly until the dough is smooth.

5 Roll out a little over half of the dough and line a 23 cm/9 inch pie plate. Fill with the salmon mixture and dampen the edges with water.

6 Roll out the remaining pastry and use to cover the pie, pinching the edges to seal. Make a cross or slash in the top of the pie for steam to escape. Re-roll any pastry trimmings and cut into fish tails or leaf shapes and use to decorate the edges of the pie, attaching them with a little beaten egg or milk. Brush more egg or milk over the rest of the pie to glaze.

7 Bake in a preheated oven, 200°C/400°F/Gas Mark 6, for 35–40 minutes until the pastry is golden. Garnish with Chinese garlic and serve hot.

Hot-smoked Trout Tart

Serves 6

INGREDIENTS

175 g/6 oz plain flour
1 tsp salt
85 g/3 oz butter, cut into
    small pieces
1 egg yolk
mixed green salad or green
    vegetable, to serve

FILLING
2 tbsp butter
1 small onion, finely chopped
1 tsp green peppercorns in brine,
    drained and roughly chopped
2 tsp stem ginger, drained
2 tsp stem ginger syrup
225 g/8 oz hot-smoked trout
    fillets, flaked

3 egg yolks
100 ml/3½ fl oz crème fraîche
100 ml/3½ fl oz double cream
1 tbsp chopped fresh parsley
1 tbsp chopped fresh chives
salt and pepper

1 Sift together the flour and salt. Rub in the butter with your fingertips until the mixture resembles coarse breadcrumbs. Add the egg yolk and enough cold water, about 2 tablespoons, to make a firm dough. Knead briefly, wrap in clingfilm and refrigerate for 30 minutes.

2 Meanwhile, make the filling. Melt the butter in a frying pan and add the onion. Cook over a low heat for 8–10 minutes until softened but not coloured. Remove from the heat and stir in the peppercorns, ginger, ginger syrup and flaked trout. Set aside.

3 Remove the pastry from the refrigerator and roll out thinly. Use to line a 23 cm/9 inch flan tin or dish. Prick the base at regular intervals with a fork. Line the pastry with foil or baking paper and baking beans. Bake in a preheated oven, 200°C/400°F/Gas Mark 6, for 12 minutes. Remove the foil or baking paper and beans and bake for a further 10 minutes until light golden and dry. Remove from the oven and allow to cool slightly. Reduce the oven temperature to 180°C/350°F/Gas Mark 4. Spread the trout mixture over the base of the pastry.

4 Mix together the egg yolks, crème fraîche, cream, parsley, chives and seasoning. Pour this mixture over the trout mixture to cover. Bake in the preheated oven for 35–40 minutes until just set and golden. Remove from the oven and allow to cool slightly before serving with a mixed green salad or green vegetable.

Smoked Haddock & Spinach Tart

Serves 6

INGREDIENTS

85 g/3 oz wholemeal flour
85 g/3 oz plain flour
pinch of salt
85 g/3 oz chilled butter, diced

FILLING
350 g/12 oz smoked
   haddock fillet
150 ml/5 fl oz milk
150 ml/5 fl oz double cream
115 g/4 oz frozen leaf
   spinach, defrosted

3 egg yolks, lightly beaten
85 g/3 oz mature Cheddar
   cheese, grated
salt and pepper

1 For the pastry, mix the flours and salt in a bowl. Rub in the butter with your fingertips until the mixture resembles fine breadcrumbs. Stir in enough cold water, about 2–3 tablespoons, to make a firm dough. Lightly knead until smooth.

2 Roll out the dough thinly and line a 20 cm/8 inch deep fluted flan tin. Put the tin in the freezer for 15 minutes. Line with foil and baking beans and bake in a preheated oven, 200°C/400°F/Gas Mark 6, for 10–12 minutes. Remove the foil and beans and bake for a further 10 minutes until pale golden and dry. Cool slightly. Reduce the oven temperature to 190°C/375°F/Gas Mark 5.

3 For the filling, place the haddock in a frying pan and add the milk and cream. Bring to the boil, cover and remove from heat. Leave for 10 minutes until the haddock is tender. Remove the fish using a slotted spoon. Strain the cooking liquid into a jug. Skin and flake the fish.

4 Squeeze the spinach to remove excess liquid. Put it in the the pastry case with the flaked fish. Add the egg yolks and 55 g/2 oz of the cheese to the fish poaching liquid and season. Mix and pour into the pastry case. Sprinkle over the remaining cheese and bake for 25–30 minutes until the filling is golden and just set.

Index

256